TRUDEAU AS STATESMAN

TRUDEAU AS STATESMAN

1965–2000

Son of Quebec, Father of Canada

MAX AND MONIQUE NEMNI
AND DAVID MILNE

DUNDURN
PRESS

Publisher: Meghan Macdonald | Acquiring editor: Russell Smith
Cover designer: Laura Boyle
Cover image: Cooper, Robert, 1951-/Library and Archives Canada/3588019

Library and Archives Canada Cataloguing in Publication

Title: Trudeau as statesman : 1965–2000, son of Quebec, father of Canada / Max and Monique Nemni and David Milne.
Names: Nemni, Max, author | Nemni, Monique, 1936-2022, author | Milne, David, 1941- author
Description: Includes bibliographical references and index.
Identifiers: Canadiana 20240537270 | ISBN 9781459755406 (softcover) | ISBN 9781459755413 (EPUB) | ISBN 9781459755420 (PDF)
Subjects: LCSH: Trudeau, Pierre Elliott. | LCSH: Prime ministers—Canada—Biography. | LCSH: Statesmen—Canada—Biography. | LCSH: Canada—Politics and government—1945- | LCGFT: Biographies.
Classification: LCC FC626.T7 N46 2025 | DDC 971.064/4092—dc23

We acknowledge the support of the Canada Council for the Arts and the Ontario Arts Council for our publishing program. We also acknowledge the financial support of the Government of Ontario, through the Ontario Book Publishing Tax Credit and Ontario Creates, and the Government of Canada.

Printed and bound in Canada.

Dundurn Press
1382 Queen Street East
Toronto, Ontario, Canada M4L 1C9
dundurn.com, @dundurnpress

Contents

PREFACE

THIS BOOK IS DEDICATED TO MONIQUE NEMNI. A JOINT AUTHOR WITH HER HUSBAND, Max, in the biographical trilogy entitled *Pierre Elliott Trudeau: Son of Quebec, Father of Canada*, she passed away suddenly on November 2, 2022, on the fourth day of a Mediterranean cruise. This was an enormous personal blow to Max after having shared seventy years of life together with Monique. It was also a terrible shock to lose his first-class author in their dream to write three books telling the story of the intellectual life of Pierre Elliott Trudeau. The third volume was then well underway, yet much remained to be written. Max was determined that his and his wife's life work together would not be forsaken. Somehow it had to be brought to completion.

While it was impossible to re-create a Monique, Max felt that he had been lucky to find an excellent replacement in David Milne, their friend and colleague in Senior College at the University of Toronto. David's extensive publications on the Trudeau years gave him a strong scholarly basis for joining the biographical team and for picking up the writing where Monique had left off. So, happily in joint authorship, Max and David pressed on with *Trudeau as Statesman* and the end of a trilogy.

Suddenly, on August 29, 2024, with the manuscript in copyedit, Max Nemni himself died from complications from pneumonia and a urinary tract infection. In his last review of the manuscript that summer, Max was exceptionally pleased. Confident that Monique and his legacy was secured with the completion of the third volume of their biographical series on Pierre Elliott Trudeau, Max had looked forward to its publication.

INTRODUCTION

WITH VOLUME THREE, WE BRING OUR BIOGRAPHY OF PIERRE ELLIOTT TRUDEAU TO ITS long-intended conclusion. Trudeau's life and thought had always had a purpose, a trajectory to which it was directed: namely, a life dedicated to the theory and practise of statesmanship. He answered its call in 1965, when at forty-six years of age, joining hands with his friends Jean Marchand and Gérard Pelletier, he plunged into federal politics. The "three wise men" were fervent Quebecers all, who had come to Ottawa in its moment of need to stave off a national crisis that they feared would break up the country. They were *of* and *from* Quebec to the depths of their souls. They would nonetheless be called *vendus* (sellouts) or *traîtres* (traitors) by their former friends and compatriots who had increasingly adopted Quebec independence as their new religion.

Philosophically, Trudeau was the best prepared of the three for this mighty task of statesmanship. As we showed in volumes one and two, he had launched himself into rigorous intellectual preparation for public office. He read and thought deeply about questions of philosophy, politics, economy, and law. Having lamented the poverty of political thought in Quebec, he had determined to remedy that defect by wholly dedicating himself to political philosophy as a foundation for politics and statesmanship. Highly idealistic and formally trained, he saw politics as a struggle over *ideas*, *rights*, and *constitutionalism*. These constituted the very foundation of good governance, which he sought to bring to his homeland of Quebec and to his country, Canada. After nearly a half century, he stood ready for public office, the political philosopher knocking on the door of political power. The question was: how would he be received?

Is an Egghead the Man for the Times?

Practical politicians had no patience for this question at all. Politics was no place for deep thinkers. What's the point of theoretical political knowledge in the gritty world of politics? Dismissed as hopeless amateurs, such was so often the fate of political theorists. And such was the reaction of professional politicians to the arrival of Pierre Trudeau in politics. Yet they turned out to be wrong. Ideas matter. Political philosophy, it turned out, could guide and drive the real world of politics.

Trudeau stood ready at last to be tested as a statesman. In this volume, we see how far he was able to see his ideas prevail in the contested world of politics — in public debate and fierce negotiation, in elections, referendums, and crisis management. How did Trudeau make the leap from political thinker to political actor? What is his political legacy? We will explore these questions as they worked themselves out in the most central battles of his political career from 1965 to 1984 and for several years afterward. Over three decades he remained a towering political figure in Canada and a well-known and respected statesman throughout the world.

No Outsider: He Lived the "Quebec Question"

In our first volume, we showed Trudeau as a separatist and revolutionary in his youth. He knew what the politics of independence felt like from the inside, from the mind of the converted. He shared the conventional thinking of his generation, and he accepted the nationalist Quebec mantle of leadership that his Jesuit teachers urged upon their students at Jean-de-Brébeuf school. He was and remained a devout Catholic, complicit with the Vatican's acceptance of fascist governments in much of pre-war Europe. After all, these were the regimes the Church urged Quebecers to admire — Mussolini, Franco, Pétain — not liberal democratic countries like Great Britain. Contrary to the myth of Trudeau always rowing against the tide of opinion as a contrarian or outsider, he thoroughly absorbed and accepted the prejudices of his place, time, and culture.

It was the same when he left Quebec and spent years abroad at Harvard University, at Sciences Po in Paris, and at the London School of Economics. Finding himself at last open to the wider world of ideas and postwar metropolitan life, he absorbed the latest thinking on modern political economy and philosophies of liberalism and socialism. As an active Catholic, Trudeau read Christian thinkers like Jacques Maritain and especially Nicolas Berdyaev, integrating spiritual values of Christianity like brotherly love into a philosophy of social justice. He read this literature carefully and critically while absorbing the main currents of thought undergirding the postwar liberal democratic world. Imbibing such ideas as readily as he had once fascist doctrines, he brought them back with him on his return to Quebec and Canada. In many ways, he turned out exactly as might be expected of a smart graduate student attending these prestigious universities, supplemented by extensive backpacking international travel.

Hence, it is not Trudeau's *exceptionalism in opinion* that should draw our attention, but rather his ready, adaptive response to the changes in the intellectual worlds around him and his *ability to change his mind.* A quick learner, brilliant, immensely disciplined, and serious in his ambition to build himself a foundation of knowledge for future statesmanship: these qualities set him apart. Once he felt he had built that intellectual foundation, it remained the job of the theorist to apply it as political actor. So, in 1965, the door opened: a call to political office came, ironically from none other than the governing party operatives in Ottawa. The egghead accepted and the rest, as they say, is history.

In the two earlier substantial volumes in this series, we carefully laid out the evolution of Trudeau's political philosophy up to the eve of his entry into politics, and we do not intend to repeat that here. Instead, we offer his ideas *in action*, as they were worked out in the heat of political combat and in the context and choices of the time. Each chapter in this volume focuses on salient issues of importance to Canada, and in each we take stock of Trudeau's actual role and impact. In all of them, we examine how far Trudeau in office was able to convert political theory into successful political practise. Equally important, we note when politics itself limited, blocked, or altered the scope of Trudeau's aspirations and achievements. At last, we come to see and bear witness to "Trudeau the statesman."

ONE

Ottawa, Here I Come!

> I shall make Statesmanship my profession and, if God permits, I shall know my profession well.
>
> P. Trudeau, Letter of Application to Harvard, 1944

ON SEPTEMBER 3, 1959, MAURICE DUPLESSIS, PREMIER OF QUEBEC, WAS IN Schefferville, deep in Quebec's North, visiting the Iron Ore Company of Canada. The undefeatable "chef" leaned on a window, smoked a cigar, and collapsed. He died four days later. His many opponents heaved a sigh of relief. He had ruled his party, the Union Nationale, with an iron fist. Although elections were held democratically, so to speak, every person and every electoral county in Quebec knew how to vote if they wanted a bridge, a highway, or a school. Through corruption, partnership with the clergy, and shrewd political skills, Duplessis had led majority governments for sixteen consecutive years. Progressive citizens hoped that without him, the Union Nationale, in disarray, would be defeated.

The election of June 22, 1960, delivered their wish. That election stands among the most significant in Quebec's history. Jean Lesage, leader of the Liberal Party, was a proud Canadian; he had been a member of the federal Liberal Party from 1945 to 1958 and had even served as a member of the

Louis St. Laurent cabinet from 1953 to 1957. He ran his campaign under the slogan "C'est l'temps que ça change!" (It's Time for Change!) His party won, securing fifty-one seats against forty-three for the Union Nationale, reaping 51.4 percent of the popular vote against 46.6 percent. Not a sweeping victory but enough. The Union Nationale had finally been defeated. In his victory speech, Lesage famously boasted: "Ladies and Gentlemen, we have crushed the infernal machine with its horrible face."

Hopes were high for all progressive voices in Canada, and in Quebec: the province had finally turned the page on the stifling era commonly known as *la grande noirceur* (the great darkness). Pierre Elliott Trudeau was overjoyed: not only was Lesage's victory good for Quebec, but, as he recalled in his *Memoirs*, he "was one of the first beneficiaries of this change."[1] Indeed, that same year, after having systematically been barred from university teaching by Duplessis and his associates, he was finally granted a professorship at the University of Montreal.

The Quiet Revolution

The Liberals embarked on an ambitious project of modernizing and secularizing Quebec. No wonder this very profound transformation has been labelled — rightly or wrongly — the "Quiet Revolution." However, as the modernization of Quebec gave a new sense of liberation to the population, it also gave birth to a new form of nationalism. This neo-nationalism had two branches. The so-called "federalist" alternative demanded that Quebec be recognized as a "distinct" society or be given a "special" or a "distinct" or even a "national" status. The other branch was outright separatist, spreading like wildfire, especially among students and intellectuals. Separatist ideology equated Quebec's plight for independence with that of colonial nations such as Algeria, with "English Canadians" being cast as the colonizers. Separatists sought "independence" — i.e., secession from Canada — pure and simple, while hoping to maintain cordial (and economic) relations with the rest of the country.

On September 10, 1960, three short months after the Liberal victory, the *Rassemblement pour l'indépendance nationale* (RIN) was founded by André d'Allemagne, Jacques Bellemare, and André Chaput, among others.

In 1961, its vice-president, Marcel Chaput, published his famous *Pourquoi je suis séparatiste*. The thirty-five thousand printed copies flew off the shelves. Translated and published a year later by Ryerson Press under the title *Why I Am a Separatist*, it shocked the nation because of both its content and its author: Chaput was a civil servant working for the Ministry of National Defence; he had perforce sworn loyalty to the Queen of Canada.

In an unusual move, and barely two years after the Liberals had toppled the Union Nationale, Lesage called for new elections to be held on November 14, 1962. The major element of the Liberal platform was the nationalization of electricity. It was vigorously proposed and defended by the bright and popular minister of natural resources, René Lévesque. Trudeau didn't feel that this move was justified "either economically or politically." But he still supported the Liberals, because all parties, he wrote, had made nationalization of electricity "wrongly or rightly a symbol of [their] virility."[2]

By then, the nationalist fervour had fully infiltrated the Liberal Party. Bending to the pressure from both outside and inside his government, Jean Lesage, the formerly staunch federalist, ran his campaign under the catchy new slogan "Maîtres chez nous" (Masters in Our House). This ambiguous message could mean that Quebecers wanted to be in control of everything pertaining to their province within the Canadian federation. But *Maîtres chez nous* could also mean that Quebecers wanted to become their sole masters, to be an independent country.

Trudeau was strongly opposed to the nationalist turn the Liberal Party was taking, but he still encouraged Quebecers to vote for it, because he couldn't fathom how any democrat could vote for any other party. To him, an alliance between the right-wing Social Credit and the Union Nationale could possibly bring them to power, a situation that had to be avoided at all costs. Furthermore, he felt that by and large the Liberals had done a good job at governing.

As political scientist Réjean Pelletier points out in his comprehensive study of Quebec's political parties, within their first few months in power, the Liberals had created several new ministries, established the Treasury Board to monitor government spending, begun to clean up the endemic patronage, instituted the principle of tenders for public works, reorganized the provincial police, and negotiated with the federal government to launch a hospital insurance scheme.[3] Impressive indeed! In two and a half years, Trudeau wrote in 1962, they had done more "than the previous government in sixteen."[4]

The Liberal Party won the November 14, 1962, election with more seats than in 1960 and with a bigger share of the popular vote. Jean Lesage continued to implement many of the reforms announced in the party's program. The Liberals put in place a skilled provincial bureaucracy and nationalized eleven privately owned electrical companies. They also substantially reformed the educational system. Up until then, education had been run by the faith-based (Catholic/Protestant) Departments of Public Instruction, with the Catholic Church fully in charge of the education of French Canadians. On May 13, 1964, a secular Ministry of Education was created. It was still formally organized on a Catholic/Protestant basis, with advisory committees (which had to approve all textbooks, among other things,) but the Catholic Church was no longer running the system. Paul Gérin-Lajoie was made Quebec's very first minister of education.

Needless to say, these reforms required money. Lots of it. Taxes were raised but could hardly suffice. The government borrowed and borrowed: between 1960 and 1966, the provincial debt rose by more than 300 percent. "Quebec's financial situation is beyond repair,"[5] wrote Pierre Godin, the well-known journalist who was René Lévesque's biographer. To find money, Lesage turned to Ottawa and fought tooth and nail to get a bigger share of the taxes. He succeeded in prying more cash from the federal government without relinquishing any provincial control. In 1965, during the federal-provincial negotiations leading to the Canada Pension Plan, he was able to secure an autonomous Quebec Pension Plan.

The Relentless Rise of Separatism

You would think that even die-hard nationalists would have rejoiced at the Liberals' gains in Ottawa. But nothing seemed to quench their thirst. Separatist movements were quickly spreading amongst francophone intellectuals, students, and artists. February 1963 saw the birth of the *Front de libération du Québec* (FLQ), an independent group advocating the "liberation" of Quebec through terrorism, a strategy hitherto unheard of in Canada. Its members didn't waste any time putting their "principles" into action: a month later, they bombed three Canadian Army barracks. In April, soon after they published their Manifesto, another of their bombs killed a night watchman. When twenty-three suspected terrorists were arrested, they got public support, and many considered them to be "political prisoners." The whole country was baffled by the news coming out of Quebec. "What does Quebec want?" wondered concerned anglophone Canadians, fearful for the country's survival.

When Lester B. Pearson became prime minister of Canada on April 8, 1963, the government was under much pressure to find a solution to this mounting threat. On July 19, he set up the Royal Commission on Bilingualism and Biculturalism — known as the B&B Commission. Its mandate was to "inquire into and report upon the existing state of bilingualism and biculturalism in Canada and to recommend what steps should be taken to develop the Canadian Confederation on the basis of an equal partnership between the two founding races."[6] It was meant to address the nationalists' severe criticism of the status of French in Canada. Instead of appeasing Quebec nationalists, it stoked their fire.

In Quebec, a "real" — as opposed to a "quiet" — revolution was the objective of *Parti pris*, a new separatist magazine launched in October 1963. On August 29, 1964, two employees of a firearms company were killed during an FLQ robbery. Outside Quebec, the hearings of the B&B Commission didn't fare well, giving rise to unbridled prejudice. The country was being torn apart. In February 1965, a preliminary report of the Commission declared: "Canada is passing through the greatest crisis in its history."[7]

The Arrival of the "Three Wise Men" in Ottawa

When Pearson called another election in 1965 in the hope of winning a majority government, Canadians expected him to find a solution to this existential crisis. As his government was also under constant attack for scandals involving Quebec cabinet ministers, he desperately needed a strong representation from this province. Jean Marchand, a prominent and popular union leader, a true liberal in the philosophical sense, and a staunch federalist, was considered the ideal choice. Marchand, who was disturbed by the rise of separatism in Quebec, was ripe for a switch into federal politics. But he was afraid of being isolated in Ottawa, so he made his conditions very clear: he wouldn't consider running unless his two friends, Gérard Pelletier and Pierre Elliott Trudeau, joined him.

Gérard Pelletier was a very well-known, popular journalist. In 1950, he had co-founded with Pierre Trudeau and others the magazine *Cité libre*, which vigorously attacked Duplessis. As a journalist for the well-respected newspaper *Le Devoir* from 1947 to 1950, his reporting of the famous Asbestos Strike had been very well received. This led him to the position of editor-in-chief of *Le Travail*, a publication of the *Confédération des travailleurs catholiques du Québec*. In 1961, he became the editor-in-chief of *La Presse*, the French-Canadian newspaper with the widest circulation in North America. However, his views put him at odds with the owners of *La Presse*, who fired him in 1964. Pelletier had never shown much interest in politics, let alone in federal matters: his forte was provincial social issues. Marchand's suggestion of going to Ottawa wouldn't have been particularly enticing to Pelletier at other times. Under the circumstances, however, it became a serious option.

Pierre Trudeau's case was totally different. Of the three, he was the only one whose interest in politics dated back to his years at the prestigious Collège Saint-Jean-de-Brébeuf. There, students were told that they were part of the elite. This gave them privileges, but also duties. They had to guide and protect their people and take an active part in their society. Young Pierre was all ears. In 1938, Trudeau, barely nineteen, wrote that those who have the aptitude for politics would "commit an act of unforgivable cowardice if they do not engage in active politics."[8] Students were also told that the long-awaited leader would emerge from their ranks. Trudeau knew he had the potential

In 1944, he wrote in his application to Harvard University: "We French-Canadians ... have too few political thinkers to lead us, and the sight of such splendid people going to ruin appalls me." This is why, he told the admissions committee: "I shall make Statesmanship my profession and, if God permits, I shall know my profession well."[9]

Back in Montreal, in 1949, he felt that there was still an important gap in his knowledge: a practical experience of the functioning of the Canadian federation. He filled it by becoming a civil servant in the Privy Council for two years. This gave him the opportunity not only to witness first-hand the daunting complexities of federal-provincial relations and of patriating the Constitution but also to delve further into the study of the British North America Act (BNA), 1867.

From the day he came back to Montreal, Trudeau had also applied himself to the analysis of the Quebec political scene. By the mid-sixties, his reputation as a brilliant scholar was well established, especially in English Canada. But he wasn't a mere theorist confined to his ivory tower; he was a man of action who didn't shun working in close collaboration with unions, occasionally standing with them on picket lines. Like Harold Laski, his famous professor at the London School of Economics, he imagined for himself a career combining impressive academic work with very active participation in the political arena. We can assume that when Marchand made his offer, Trudeau was overjoyed at this opportunity.

If Trudeau and Pelletier were ready to join the Liberal Party, the federal Liberal Party wasn't rejoicing at all at the prospect. Neither were the Quebec Liberals. On hearing the news, the Quebec premier, Jean Lesage, "urged Pearson to persuade Marchand to get 'real' professionals with him.... He was contemptuous of Pierre Trudeau and Gérard Pelletier. 'You don't take people like that and put them in politics. You need professionals. Not dilettantes. Not deep thinkers'"[10] Great efforts were deployed to dissuade them from running. As late as the eve of the news conference announcing their candidacy, Quebec MPs Guy Favreau and Maurice Lamontagne tried for four hours to convince the two not to run.[11]

Of Trudeau and Pelletier, which did the federal Liberals loathe more? It depends on whose recollections you read. Pearson was sure it was Pelletier. He wrote: "While Pierre Trudeau had made some pretty tough speeches about nuclear arms and about myself in the context, Pelletier had been writing editorials day after day about the inequity of the Liberal regime."[12] René Lévesque told it differently in his *Memoirs*. He recalled being with Maurice Sauvé — the minister of forestry in Pearson's cabinet — when Marchand told Sauvé on the phone, "I've just come from seeing Pearson, and things aren't going too well.... They're dying to get me. They're ready to take Pelletier, too. But as far as Trudeau is concerned, it's no soap. In their eyes he's nothing but a little drawing-room socialist who had the nerve not so long ago to call them a bunch of idiots."[13]

Whose recollections are closer to the truth? Documents from that period seem to indicate that Pearson's later admiration for and trust in Trudeau may have embellished his recollection of Trudeau's scathing criticism of the party, and of his own stand on nuclear arms. Indeed, many Quebec Liberals hadn't forgotten that Trudeau had once used, among other derogatory words, the term "trained idiots."[14] In "Pearson ou l'abdication de l'esprit" (Pearson or the Abdication of Integrity),[15] Trudeau had accused Pearson of yielding to pressure from the U.S. government and flip-flopping on prior Liberal Party policy rejecting nuclear weapons in Canada, solely for political advantage in the 1963 election against John Diefenbaker's government. He boldly wrote: "Power was offered to Mr. Pearson, who had nothing to lose, save his honour. He lost it, and so did the rest of the party."[16] It is easy to see why Martin Sullivan wrote in *Mandate '68*: "Many Liberals, when they finished reading the article, put *Cité libre* down with a vow that never, while there was a breath in their bodies, would Pierre Elliott Trudeau ever be considered as a Liberal candidate."[17]

But Jean Marchand was unshakable. It was a package deal; take it or leave it. They took it, and the Liberals started looking for safe ridings for those who came to be called "les trois colombes" (the three wise men; literal translation: the three doves). Ridings for Marchand and Pelletier were easily found, but getting one for Trudeau presented a real challenge. As Sullivan put it, he "possessed every drawback a Quebec politician could have. He was unknown, unconventional, and unmarried. Moreover, he was an intellectual and was believed to have radical left-wing tendencies.... It was now clear to the party that he would be unacceptable in a French-Canadian riding, and awfully hard to sell in an English one."[18]

Sullivan wasn't quite right about Trudeau being unknown. He was well known in academic circles across Canada, especially in English Canada. But, true enough, he was unknown to the general public. Yet in Quebec he was all too well known to separatists and nationalists, his sworn enemies. It was easy to foresee that they would do their best to jeopardize his chances of being elected anywhere in Quebec.

The party finally settled on Mount Royal, a strong Liberal riding with an important Anglophone and Jewish population. Twice Trudeau nearly dropped out of the race. First, he didn't want to run against Victor Goldbloom to win the nomination. Goldbloom was "a good man," he told Marchand. Marchand convinced him to stay. Again, when he learned that as the Liberal candidate, he would have to fight against the NDP contestant, Charles Taylor, a friend for whom he had campaigned in the previous election, he wanted to pack it in. And again Marchand intervened and won over the reluctant candidate.

The federal election of November 8, 1965, was a big disappointment for Liberals, who were returned once more as a minority government. It did, however, send the Three Wise Men to Ottawa, two of them arriving through the back door, so to speak. Jean Marchand was immediately given the ministry of citizenship and immigration. Pierre Trudeau and Gérard Pelletier were to take their seats as back benchers. That didn't last long, not for Trudeau anyway. He hadn't even had time to enjoy a European break before Pearson offered him a position as his parliamentary secretary. Reached in Europe, his first reaction was to refuse the offer because he didn't feel ready: he hadn't yet set foot in the House of Commons. How could he be successful when he hadn't had time to find his bearings? But Marchand insisted: the three of them had come to Ottawa to play an active role in politics. Trudeau couldn't bypass the opportunity offered him on a silver platter. And so, he didn't.

Meanwhile, in Quebec, things were not settling down. On May 24, 1965, the separatist magazine *Parti pris* organized a demonstration to protest the celebration of Queen Victoria. The gathering of about two thousand people eventually turned ugly and led to a confrontation with the police. Shop windows were broken, a police car was set on fire, and hundreds of arrests were made. On Canada Day, a violent demonstration in Lafontaine Park, in the eastern part of Montreal, ended with 105 arrests. The same day, in the western part of Montreal, a bomb exploded outside Westmount City Hall. In both instances, the FLQ was the primary suspect. On May 5, 1966, one more person was killed in a shoe factory by yet another FLQ bomb. Two weeks later, another bomb exploded on Parliament Hill, killing its carrier. On June 3, dynamite sticks placed in cigarette packages exploded at the Paul Sauvé Arena during the last electoral campaign of the provincial Liberal Party.[19]

The Quiet Revolution wasn't so quiet anymore. Canadians, shaken by these repeated and unprecedented acts of violence, became more and more apprehensive about the future of the country. Quebecers were turning their backs on the Canadian federation. Even the federalist Lesage was promoting Quebec's autonomy on the international scene. On February 27, 1965, the Quebec minister of education, Paul Gérin-Lajoie, signed a co-operative agreement with France regarding education. Although education fell under provincial jurisdiction, international agreements were the prerogative of the federal government. The federal government was well aware that acting autonomously on the international scene could pave the way to independence. Quebec's bold moves were encouraged by Charles de Gaulle, who was delighted at the prospect of France acquiring a foothold in North America. Premier Jean Lesage and his ministers were received like heads-of-state in Paris. On November 24, 1965, a Quebec-France cultural entente was signed between the two governments.

When the election set for June 5, 1966, was called, Lesage and his party were sure that Quebecers, including nationalists, would be quite satisfied with their record and that their re-election would be a shoo-in. So was the media. In fact, the press considered the Union Nationale to be such an insignificant opposition that they focused their critiques on the Liberals. This upset the government, but the media strongly believed that there was no danger in doing so, since they saw the re-election of Lesage and his team as a mere formality. Yet, on June 5, the inconceivable happened. While, at 8:30 p.m., Radio-Canada predicted the re-election of Lesage and his Liberal government, half an hour later, at 9:00 p.m., it announced the victory of Daniel Johnson, the leader of the Union Nationale. The Union Nationale? The party associated with patronage, corruption, authoritarianism? The party against which progressive intellectuals had fought tooth and nail? Trudeau was aghast.

Granted, it wasn't an outright victory: Johnson did get five more seats than Lesage, but the Liberals had won the popular vote (47.4 percent against 40.9 percent). Journalists asked Daniel Johnson why he thought the Liberals had won the popular vote. He attributed much of that to the votes of Anglophones and Jews.[20] About thirty years later, a distraught Jacques Parizeau, premier of Quebec and leader of the PQ, would attribute his loss of the 1995 referendum to "money and the ethnic vote," money being the code word for Jews and English-speaking Quebecers.

Constitutional Roulette with Separatism

As prime minister, Pearson had to come to grips with the constitutional challenges posed by Quebec nationalism in all its dangerous forms. In January 1967, he convened a group of experts to closely examine the Canadian Constitution. The group was headed by his parliamentary secretary, Pierre Trudeau, and managed by Jean Beetz, a former colleague of Trudeau at the University of Montreal, and now head of the federal-provincial secretariat in the Privy Council. On April 4, 1967, the parliamentary secretary, Pierre Trudeau, became minister of justice.

That same month, John Robarts, premier of Ontario, announced that his government would hold a provincial premiers constitutional conference on November 27, 1967. The federal government couldn't let Ontario convene such a conference without reacting. Pearson issued his own invitation to a federal-provincial constitutional conference to be held in Ottawa from February 5 to 7, 1968. Pierre Trudeau was put in charge of the position paper of the government.

On May 18, 1967, Robarts presented to the Ontario Legislature a resolution to hold a provincial premiers conference on November 27, 1967, to assess Quebec's place in the federation and consider whatever adjustments were needed in the Canadian Constitution. Labelled "Confederation for Tomorrow Conference," it was approved almost unanimously (seventy to one).[21] In his opening remarks, Robarts acknowledged that his initiative had drawn some criticism. One could still wonder, as did Steve Paikin, fifty years later: "Why would John Robarts, a unilingual anglophone from London, Ontario, who had a progressive conservative caucus filled with guys who were basically loyal to the orange lodge [who] didn't care for French

Catholics or French speaking people at all.... Why was this such a big deal to him?"[22] Wasn't he doing it for political gain? Paikin asked these questions in a televised interview with Charles Beer, then Ontario federal-provincial affairs secretary. Beer's reply was that Robarts had a genuine interest in French Canadians' plight for the survival of their language and culture in Quebec as in all of Canada.[23]

While we agree that Robarts had a genuine interest in protecting the French language, there are other reasons that explain his association with Quebec. More specifically, he saw an opportunity to reform the Constitution in a more decentralized manner. Provinces had always clamoured for more powers. When Robarts presented his resolution, he asserted that after one hundred years, "an overall reappraisal of the federal structure is essential." But if the Constitution needed a serious reappraisal, was it appropriate for a province to call and hold a constitutional conference? Traditionally, it was the federal government that called first ministers together for discussions regarding matters affecting the whole country. The Constitution was undoubtedly one of these. This was a first in Canadian history. At any rate, Robarts held the conference and sent an invitation to Pearson, who, unsurprisingly, did not attend the meeting. The premiers were happy he didn't come. As Charles Beer recalled, they were able to talk a lot more freely about everything. As for Daniel Johnson and the Quebec government, they saw this as an incredible opportunity to speak to a much broader Canadian audience.

In the position paper Johnson brought with him to the premiers' conference, he described the BNA Act as "An Impotent Constitution" to be discarded. The new one should provide for massive decentralization:

> All provinces would, at the outset, be granted identical constitutional powers. Once the provinces had acquired all the powers that Quebecers needed in order to achieve their dreamed nation — in "international relations, culture, manpower, and the administration of justice" — the other provinces could cede them back to Ottawa if they wished.[24]

In the final analysis, the premiers agreed on no specific resolution. They emphasized, however, the necessity to hold more conferences to discuss the reform of the Constitution to improve the balance in the distribution of powers between the two levels of government. Johnson was delighted: his demand for much greater decentralization held an undeniable appeal for all premiers, and he had found a strong ally in Robarts. Furthermore, his views had reached a very large audience. For the first time in Canadian history, this provincial conference, transmitted live, could be viewed by all Canadians in the privacy of their homes, thanks to an amazing new medium: television. A few months later, the federal-provincial conference of February 1968 would also be televised.

Expo 67 and the Charles de Gaulle Affair

While politicians were struggling with the crisis threatening Canadian unity, happier thoughts were on the minds of other Canadians: in 1967, Canada would be one hundred years old! All sorts of celebrations with great panache were to mark its centennial. Pierre Berton, the well-known historian, author, and media personality, wrote a book entitled *1967: The Last Good Year* (in paperback *1967: The Turning Point.*) Although 1967 wasn't really — as Berton suggested in his first title — the last good year, it turned out to be a crucial year in Canadian history and a turning point. Modest, unassuming Canada was going to show the world what it could do. According to the historian Gary Miedema, "Massive in scope and daunting in size, the centennial celebrations were without doubt the most comprehensive, expensive and extravagant nationalist project ever undertaken by the Canadian state."[25]

The 1967 International and Universal Exposition, or Expo 67, as it is commonly known, was the highlight of the festivities. Held in Montreal from April 27 to October 29, 1967, it is considered the most successful World's Fair of the twentieth century, with the most attendees and sixty-two nations participating. It also set the single-day attendance record for a World's Fair, with 569,500 visitors on its third day.

As Canadians were eagerly preparing for this great event, so was Daniel Johnson. He was sure that if he could bypass Ottawa and have Charles de

Gaulle attend Expo as a guest of Quebec, he would greatly boost his position on the international scene. He decided to deliver the invitation personally. On May 17 he arrived in Paris, where he was received like a head of state. He beseeched France to support French Canadians in their struggle against the Anglo-Saxon hegemony in North America. His plea must have struck a sensitive chord with the president, who harboured grandiose ambitions for France. De Gaulle accepted the invitation. *Mission accomplie.*

Protocol required that, should De Gaulle arrive by plane, he would have to land in Ottawa. To avoid this thorny issue, the *Général* crossed the Atlantic on the cruiser ship *Colbert.* On July 23, he disembarked in full regalia in Quebec City, where he was greeted by an enthusiastic crowd, five thousand strong. In the evening, during an official dinner at the Château Frontenac, he declared that he was witnessing "the advent of a people who wished, in every field, to determine their own future and take their destiny in their own hands. France salutes this accession with all her soul."[26]

Daniel Johnson and De Gaulle took the symbolically charged Chemin du Roy to reach Montreal. All along the way, De Gaulle repeatedly told the cheering crowds that France stood behind French Quebecers' struggle for emancipation. At some point, he even compared Quebec's ultimate liberation to the liberation of France from the Nazis in 1944: "I will tell you a secret which you must not repeat. This evening, here, and all along my route, I found myself in an atmosphere no different from that of *la libération.*" As we know, De Gaulle's provocative statements culminated in the famous and unforgettable "Vive le Québec libre!" shout from the balcony of Montreal City Hall. This, of course, was the rallying cry of the FLQ. The crowd, estimated at fifteen thousand, went wild.

The federal government was outraged. But how should Pearson react? During the cabinet meeting of July 25, some, like Jean Marchand, Robert Winters, and the senior minister Paul Martin, feared that a strong rebuttal would add fuel to the fire. Pierre Trudeau, who was sworn in as minister of justice on April 4, totally disagreed. He was convinced that a lack of response from the federal government would be interpreted as a sign of weakness.[27] Pearson was swayed by Trudeau's arguments. That evening, on television, the prime minister declared De Gaulle's interference with Canadian affairs "unacceptable." Furthermore, he said, "the people of Canada are free. Every province of Canada is free. Canadians do not need to be liberated. Indeed, many thousands of Canadians gave their lives in two world wars in the liberation of France and other European countries."[28]

De Gaulle's sole response was to cancel his trip to Ottawa. His departure did not put an end to the polemics and emotional reactions that his use of the FLQ slogan had unleashed. Whereas in other provinces people were mostly outraged, a poll conducted by CROP revealed that 60 percent of Quebecers did not blame De Gaulle for his interference in Canadian affairs, and 50 percent believed that Ottawa had reacted too harshly.[29] On August 12, in the Quebec legislative assembly, Johnson tabled a motion to "thank General de Gaulle for coming to Quebec ... and to reprimand the federal government whose actions prevented him from completing his trip to Canada."[30] To this day, the controversy surrounding de Gaulle's interference in Canadian affairs has not died down. Numerous studies have been published on this subject, with conflicting interpretations. Yet, De Gaulle's most famous — or infamous — exclamation doubtless advanced the separatist agenda.[31]

A Justice Minister Takes Centre Stage

Pierre Trudeau's star was surely rising. Lester Pearson had given him the responsibility of preparing the government's constitutional position for the February 1968 conference. Pierre Trudeau would carry the mantle of federal authority in opposition to Quebec nationalist leaders and tag-along premiers. But meanwhile, he was already boldly making a name for himself with another big dossier, one that could easily have put an end to his career in politics. As the newly appointed justice minister, he had taken on a heroic project — namely, the audacious attempt to amend the Criminal Code on a troika of sensitive, if not explosive, subjects — homosexuality, divorce, and abortion. Whatever drove him to invest himself in an undertaking that seasoned politicians wouldn't have touched with a ten-foot pole?

In truth, when canvassing his options with senior officials in the department, he had been advised to take a cautious, safer route. He would have none of it. He preferred to tackle the most daunting subjects even in the face of adamant opposition from most religious authorities. Despite his deep Catholic faith, Trudeau insisted on separating private matters of faith or morality from public crimes. He could scarcely have chosen more hotly contested issues, though in every case criminal law was severely affecting the lives and liberties of Canadians. In his view, criminal law should not unfairly intrude into or constrain the private lives of the Canadian people. A just society is a *liberal* society that keeps the state within its proper bounds.

The question of homosexuality arose sharply with the case of Everett George Klippert. In 1960, this Calgary bus driver was convicted of eighteen counts of gross indecency for having consensual sex with other men. For this, he was sentenced to four years in prison. In 1965, he was convicted again, in the Northwest Territories, on four additional charges of gross indecency. This brought him three more years in prison, leading to his possible designation as a dangerous sex offender and life imprisonment. The man had never attacked anyone nor been accused of having anything other than consensual sex. Why was he *dangerous*? What was the definition of a dangerous sex offender?

In the fifties and early sixties, during the Cold War, homosexuals were suspected of endangering national security because of their vulnerability to blackmail. Hysterical campaigns were launched against them.[32] Pressure was put on the government to label them "dangerous" in order to prevent them from holding any public office. Bending to the pressure, in 1961, the Conservative government of John Diefenbaker had changed the definition of "dangerous sex offender" to include anyone who was likely to re-offend after committing a sexual offence. In Klippert's case, the two psychiatrists who examined him declared him to be neither a pedophile nor inclined to violence, but that he was likely to seek out sex with men upon his release.

Consequently, the Court had no choice but to designate him a dangerous sex offender. In March 1966, he was sentenced to an indefinite period of detention. The case went to the Supreme Court. On November 7, 1967, in a three-to-two decision, the Court dismissed Klippert's appeal. The press, some members of Parliament, and many Canadians were outraged. Dissenting Justice John Cartwright pointedly suggested that if applied, such rulings "would bring about serious overcrowding in the nation's prisons."[33]

So, the case arrived on the desk of the new justice minister, Pierre Trudeau. He seized the opportunity to shake off the dust accumulated on a range of such antiquated laws affecting divorce, homosexuality, and abortion. He proposed immediate reforms in Omnibus Bill 150. All three topics struck a raw nerve because they went to the heart of many religious beliefs and values. This was particularly so for the Catholic Church, which had had a remarkable stronghold on Quebec society until the early 1960s. Some religions accepted the principle of divorce, but homosexuality and abortion were — and still are for many religious people — considered to be very serious sins. How could he reconcile a change in these laws with his own deep personally held beliefs? The answer lies in his political philosophy.

On December 21, 1967, in a scrum in the House of Commons, Trudeau famously declared that "there's no place for the state in the bedrooms of the nation." This ringing declaration was his recasting of *Globe and Mail* correspondent Martin O'Malley's earlier remark that "the state had no right or duty to creep into the bedrooms of the nation."[34] Hence, in that spirit, consensual same-sex acts in private by adults twenty-one years of age or older should not be the concern of the country's criminal law. Trudeau strongly believed in the separation of church and state and made an important distinction between a sin and a crime. According to this principle, sins are a personal matter, which may differ from one religion to another or from one morality to another. These are best dealt with by the respective religious authorities or by the individual's conscience. Crimes, on the other hand, are matters of public concern that belong by their very nature in the law and engage the state's judicial system. Consequently, the state should not confuse the two. To paraphrase the *Globe and Mail* editorial of December 12, 1967, Trudeau set out "to unlock the locked step of law and morality."

Applying that distinction to homosexuality was a very tall order in 1967, with no gay liberation movement anywhere in sight. Even now, more than a half century later, at least seventy countries around the world still treat homosexuality as a crime. At the time, and until 1973, the American Psychiatric Association considered homosexuality a pathological disease. Many faith-based moralists still consider it wicked and sinful. But does this mean that it should be treated as a crime? A year after Trudeau started the proceedings to change the criminal law, opinions were still divided: only 42 percent of Canadians agreed in a Gallup poll that homosexual behaviour between two consenting adults aged twenty-one or older should not be a criminal act, whereas 41 percent of respondents considered such behaviour criminal.

In 2016, William Thorsell, former editor-in-chief of the *Globe and Mail*, recalled his distress as a young adolescent when he realized in 1963 that "to be gay was to be a social pariah, a 'criminal sexual psychopath' under the Criminal Code, a cast-out from religion and 'psychologically disordered' in medical parlance."[35] Innumerable similar traumatic recollections have been published in recent years in Canada and around the world. On November 28, 2017, Prime Minister Justin Trudeau's public apology to LGBTQ people listed some of their former sufferings: "It is our collective shame that Canadians who identify as lesbian, gay … were unjustly treated — fired from jobs, denied promotions, surveyed, arrested, convicted, and vindictively shamed because of their sexual orientation. People lost their livelihoods, their families, and some, their lives."

Canada was influenced by the American treatment of homosexuality. Gary Kinsman, a prominent Canadian sociologist and expert on LGBTQ issues, noted that in the McCarthy era, many people thought that homosexuals were "enemies of society in general who become enemies of capitalism in particular. Without being necessarily Marxist they serve the end of the Communist International in the name of their rebellion against the prejudices, standards, ideals of the 'bourgeois' world." McCarthy "figured that if he got his hands on a homosexual, he had his hands on a communist."[36] In national security discourse, homosexuality was sometimes portrayed "as a virus sweeping across the continent."[37] Homosexuals were even more vulnerable in Canada. An article reprinted in the *Civil Service News* in 1956 revealed that following the Gouzenko spy affair in 1946, during St. Laurent's term as justice minister, "there [was] less concern than in the United States about the rights of individuals involved. To Canadian officials, the safety of the state [came] first."[38]

On December 21, 1968, Pierre Trudeau introduced in the House of Commons Bill 150 (omnibus bill), part of which decriminalized homosexual acts in private between two consenting adults twenty-one years of age or older. His startling declaration about the bedrooms of the nation was electrifying. The sentence caught fire, propelled Trudeau to stardom, and signalled a generational shift in Canadian politics.

It also triggered a formidable backlash. On December 22, in response to the proposed bill, Calgary police chief Ken McIver described homosexuality as "a horrible, vicious and terrible thing. Decriminalizing it would represent decay in Canadian society."[39] Quebec provincial secretary Yves Gabias agreed that it would lead to decadence.[40] The debate raged until the bill was adopted, and beyond. The fierce opposition came from members of the Progressive Conservative Party and from Créditistes in Quebec. The Créditiste MPs, led by Réal Caouette, were so opposed to the changes relating to homosexuality and abortion that they held up the debate for three weeks. They argued that communism, socialism, and atheism were behind the changes. René Matte found it scandalous "to see representatives of the people being obliged to discuss these questions." The Créditistes demanded that a public referendum be held on these issues. As we will see later, these vicious attacks hounded Trudeau throughout his campaign for the federal election of June 25, 1968.

Respecting divorce, there was scarcely any doubt that many Canadians were locked into doomed marriages with little escape under the country's highly restrictive grounds for divorce. As Professor F.J.E. Jordan pointed out: "In the very important areas of matrimonial relations, namely, divorce and capacity to marry, a reluctant Parliament had left the people with laws and practices much better suited to the Victorian age in which they had been enacted."[41] Indeed, prior to 1968, there was no uniform federal divorce law in Canada. In Quebec and Newfoundland, it was simple: there were none. In these provinces, people who wanted to divorce had to seek the passage of a private act of Parliament. Elsewhere, different laws applied in different provinces, and in many cases, these dated back to the United Kingdom Matrimonial Causes Act of 1857. According to this double-standard law, a husband could obtain divorce on the grounds of his wife's adultery. For the wife, adultery of the husband didn't provide sufficient grounds for divorce: she had to establish "that her husband had committed incestuous adultery, rape, sodomy, bestiality, bigamy, or adultery coupled with cruelty or desertion."[42] As MP Andrew Brewin reminded members of Parliament, "The archaic divorce laws we have had have caused untold misery to many thousands of Canadians. This measure of reform is long overdue."[43]

Seeking to bring Canadian law into closer conformity to current society, Trudeau proposed that the grounds for divorce be broadened to include cruelty, adultery, long-term separation, and the like. Marc Lalonde, a long-time friend and collaborator, then senior advisor to Pearson, warned Trudeau of the enormous risk he was taking by wanting to reform the divorce law. If he succeeded, the upside would be enormous. But it could also become an ugly, divisive, and career-ending enterprise.[44] Trudeau still pushed ahead.

The changes to the divorce law were introduced in a separate piece of legislation: Bill C-187. Unsurprisingly, much of the opposition to the proposed Bill came from conservative Catholic Quebecers for whom marriage was indissoluble. To give but one example, Alcide Simard, MP from Lac-Saint-Jean, opposed the bill on the grounds that "a marriage essentially admits of an absolute and irrevocable bond of faithfulness. Legal tolerance for divorce is ... a social ill which is contaminating an entire nation. The state must make divorce very difficult, otherwise it seems to condone it. If part of the population has lost all natural sense of morality, the lawmakers must show some instead."[45]

The Canadian Catholic Conference — the national organization of Catholic Bishops of Canada — took a hard line on divorce. In their view, liberalizing the law could result in "problems more serious than those it seeks to control."[46] They felt that it did not sufficiently protect the family, and in particular the well-being of children caught in a divorce. Trudeau told Parliament that the purpose of the law was not to undermine the family as an institution, but to make husbands and wives equal before the law.

The new law established a uniform principle across Canada. It removed the existing double standard by recognizing the same grounds for divorce for husbands and wives. It expanded the fault-based grounds from adultery to include, among other factors, mental or physical cruelty and addiction to alcohol or drugs. It also added new grounds, including separation for three years resulting from permanent breakdown of the marriage. The debates went on; some criticized the new law for going too far, others for not going far enough.

Trudeau agreed that the law wasn't perfect; it was a pragmatic solution to an urgent problem. It went as far as it could without embarking on a prolonged process of federal-provincial consultations. He asked the members of the House of Commons: "Should the government wait for one year or perhaps several years to produce a bill closer to perfection, or should it act as soon as possible and attempt to introduce the best possible bill under our jurisdiction and … undertake negotiations later which eventually may lead to improving the law?"[47]

On December 19, the last long day of the debate, Bill C-187 was passed. Members of the House gave Trudeau a standing ovation. It became law in June 1968. To some extent, the many interviews and media reports on the proposed reforms of the Criminal Code ended up being more about the justice minister than the bill. Reporters and viewers were fascinated by the man and his message. On December 10, Barbara Amiel, host of CBC Television's public affairs show *The Way It Is*, introduced Trudeau as "the young, eligible, rich, handsome, and bachelor minister of justice."[48] He went from being hardly known outside Quebec to becoming the Liberal minister to watch.

Divorce was the "easy" reform; abortion was a nightmare. At that time, any step taken to cause an abortion was an offence liable to life imprisonment. The mere word "abortion" still sends shivers down many spines, in very militant pro-life as well as pro-choice camps. While doing our research at the Robarts Library, we came across *The Politics of Abortion*, published in 1992. Some pages were cut with a razor; many others were smeared with red ink, or marked with vulgar comments such as: "Shit, stop fucking if you don't want kids" or "Baby killer."[49] In *Heresy: The Ten Lies They Spread About Christianity*, best-selling author Michael Coren argued that a woman does have the freedom to do what she wants with her body, provided she does not "tamper with or kill a distinct person within her."[50] He didn't, at that point in his political evolution, accept any abortion, not even in cases of rape or incest.

Pro-choice advocates saw it very differently. Marilyn Wilson, former executive director of Canadian Abortion Rights Action League, claims that not only should women have the right to control their bodies, but the illegality of abortion has never stopped its widespread use. "Illegal abortions were common, but often of poor safety. Several hundred women per year died from botched abortions."[51] Pregnant daughters of the rich were sent to reliable physicians who did abortions for cash. It is estimated that these physicians did twenty to thirty abortions per week. Women who were not rich were left to do it themselves or with the help of an untrained abortionist. The mortality rate was high and the infection rate over 50 percent.

Now, more than half a century later, the fight still rages on. One can imagine how divisive such a reform must have been in 1967. MPs' opinions ranged from wanting to ban abortion outright to granting women abortion on demand. Even the government's standing committee on health and welfare couldn't reach a consensus because of their conflicting opinions.[52] The far-right religious journal *Vers demain* accused Trudeau of "legalizing the murder of innocent human beings." Créditistes MPs staged a filibuster of Parliament over the amendments concerning abortion.[53] Faced with such a contentious issue, Trudeau adopted a middle-of-the-road reform, declaring, "We've gone about as far as we dared."[54]

On May 14, 1969, Omnibus Bill C-150, which included an amendment to section 251 of the Criminal Code prohibiting abortions, was adopted by the House of Commons. By then, Trudeau was prime minister, and John Turner was the minister of justice. The law made abortions legal when the health of the woman was in danger, as determined by a three-doctor hospital committee. The term "health" was purposely not defined. These committees were free to determine when a danger to the woman's "health" (including psychological health) would justify a therapeutic abortion.

Trudeau Joyfully Rides the Waves of Politics

As a newly minted politician in his first few years, Trudeau coolly threw himself into hornets' nests. And he came out largely whole, slightly stung yet made strong in controversy. His brave and successful law reforms brought Parliament to its feet in standing ovation. The doubters, the old guard, had clearly not taken the measure of the man. But much more lay ahead — deep existential threats to the future of Canada — and these too were placed on the desk of this rising justice minister. Would his remedies pass the test of time? Moving ever closer to centre stage, he was destined to make his mark upon the whole country. A young man who had once dreamed himself a statesman would now find his dearest wish fulfilled.

TWO

Two Nations or One?

PIERRE TRUDEAU COULD SCARCELY BELIEVE THAT HE WOULD CROSS SWORDS WITH Premier Daniel Johnson, lacklustre head of the old, once discredited Union Nationale, in the upcoming federal-provincial conference of February 5–7, 1968. The nightmare of *la grande noirceur* (the great darkness) had returned, come back from the grave, *duplessisme* reincarnated in the Quebec election of 1966. It was an astonishing turn of events. But it made his work as justice minister easier. He could focus on his old nemesis, now slyly adapting its ideology and party platform to the nationalist context of the time.

In just four years, the Union Nationale had transformed itself from a grotesque circus, *un cirque grotesque*, under a "calamity" named Daniel Johnson, in its 1961 convention, to modern success in 1965. The party had moved away from the old boozy secrecy and had opened to the press and the public. But at the heart of the party transformation lay a book, ghost-written for Daniel Johnson and published expressly for the convention, with the tantalizing title *Égalité ou indépendance* (Equality or Independence). It took on and upstaged Lesage's *Maîtres chez nous*, flagrantly raising for the first time in Quebec party politics a real choice of independence for Quebecers. Stealing the nationalist thunder, the policy's only alternative option (*Égalité*) presented Canada with a *two-nations* offer, a joint binational restructuring of power between Quebec and the "ROC,"* a thing called English Canada. Take it or leave it. This was no small threat — but a delicious ultimatum. What cheek from *la belle province* — now an imagined nation, equal to all the rest! The document was, of course, unanimously adopted by the two thousand delegates to the convention.

Who could not "catch the drift"? As symbolism, *Égalité* was crystal clear. Yet whatever did it *really* mean? In truth, it floated in veiled ambiguity. Which choice was the government proposing? Not even Daniel Johnson knew where he stood: one moment he spoke for independence, the next, against. In its cunning evasiveness, the policy wanted to have it both ways — in effect, to win both sides of the argument. No one who endorsed it could know what its adoption would mean, but it sure felt good to demand "big changes or else." This posture suited Daniel Johnson just fine. He would take the veiled threat forward and demand a transfer of powers to Quebec "at all levels: cultural, social, and economic"[1] so that its people could finally have its homeland.

The Spectre of Two Nations

Johnson was at the high point of his career. His notion of a "two nations" Canada was steadily gaining ground. The federal New Democratic Party formally adopted it in the early sixties, much to Trudeau's dismay, and he accused the party of playing right into the separatists' hands. At their national convention in July 1967, the party backed away from its two nations policy, only to flip then to the phrase "special status for Quebec." Meanwhile, federal Liberals under the leadership of Lester B. Pearson seemed to be granting *de facto* special status for Quebec by their many concessions to Lesage in the name of "co-operative federalism." Where, thought Trudeau, did progressives think they were going? As for the Progressive Conservative Party, at their "Thinkers' Conference" in Quebec City in 1967, participants, swayed by keynote speaker Marcel Faribault, resolved: "That Canada is composed of two founding peoples" (translated in French as *deux nations*). Playing with the ambiguities of translation, Daniel Johnson's "two nations" policy scarcely seemed to meet much opposition among federal political parties.

* ROC, literally "Rest of Canada," became the inglorious phantom partner imagined into being by Quebec nationalists as a reverse mirror image — a centralized English alter ego — of Quebec itself.

The situation was no less worrisome in Quebec. Separatist and nationalist voices were clamouring for independence or, at the very least, for some form of "distinct society," while federalists had no champions for their cause. *Cité libre*, known for its relentless attacks on the separatist ideology, had suspended its publication shortly after Trudeau and Pelletier had gone to Ottawa.[2] Unchallenged, the separatist ideology was sweeping the province, infiltrating even the highest ranks of the purportedly federalist Quebec Liberal Party, now sitting in opposition. Their nationalist slogan, *Maîtres chez nous*, had been outflanked by Daniel Johnson's *Egalité ou indépendance*. How could they get back to power in an increasingly nationalist Quebec?

Quebec Liberal discussions were going nowhere until René Lévesque, the former and very popular minister of natural resources, found what he believed to be the Achilles heel of Johnson's demand for equality. Equality is impossible without independence, he claimed. Even if Quebec were recognized as a nation, and got many additional and exclusive powers, it would still be "exposed to all the traps that were being set for it in Ottawa and elsewhere."[3] So why stop at this half-baked solution? To Lévesque, sovereignty, coupled with an "association" with the rest of Canada, was the only logical path to full emancipation. Note the word "sovereignty" (*souveraineté*). Why not "independence"? The answer lay in Lévesque's refusal to use the same language adopted by radical, and sometimes violent, groups, such as Pierre Bourgault's RIN (*Rassemblement pour l'indépendance nationale*). Jean Lesage was totally opposed to Lévesque's proposal, but he let him present it at their congress of October 14, 1967. When, by a margin of 1,500 votes against 7, the party adopted "special status," proposed by Paul Gérin-Lajoie, rather than "sovereignty-association," a disgruntled Lévesque severed all ties with the party.

News of Lévesque's latest position on "sovereignty" had spread before the congress. Johnson, who was ambivalent about independence, seized this opportunity to distance himself from Lévesque's extreme position. In an interview with *La Presse*, held in Hawaii, where Johnson was recovering from some health issues, the premier declared: "In June 1966, the Union Nationale had not received a mandate to construct a Chinese wall around Quebec." On the contrary, Johnson merely demanded "a new Canadian constitution, made in Canada, by Canadians and for Canadians, by virtue of which every citizen, French-speaking or English-speaking, regardless of ethnic origin, would feel at home everywhere in Canada."[4] This new statement delighted the federal government. Pearson joyfully declared: "We are very happy to learn that M. Johnson doesn't want to isolate Quebec."[5] Pierre Trudeau told the House of Commons on October 5: "We are happy that he is finally coming around to our point of view."[6] He added that he had always maintained that one should first fully take advantage of what is already in the Constitution before rejecting it.

Meanwhile, as news spread about Lévesque's promotion of independence, money started to flow out of the province. On November 3, 1967, Jacques Parizeau, then economic advisor to the government, and later Quebec premier, publicly maintained that the so-called flight of capital attributed to Lévesque's sovereignty stance was both exaggerated and unfounded.[7] On November 19, 1967 — barely a week before the Confederation for Tomorrow Conference to be held in Toronto — René Lévesque launched *Le mouvement souveraineté-association* (MSA). It immediately gave the independence option a tremendous boost and a new respectability in nationalist circles.[8] In January 1968, a month before the federal-provincial conference, Lévesque published his remarkably successful *Option Québec*. Membership in the MSA soared from seven hundred in January to seven thousand in April.

And just as the premiers were heading for Toronto, another event gave still more ammunition to Johnson's constitutional demands. From November 23 to 26, 1967, a conference was held in Montreal under the ominous title *Les États généraux du Canada français*. Any francophone would have learned at school that les *États généraux* (Estates General) of 1789 had led to the French Revolution. The message was loud and clear: Canada beware! We could be on our way to independence. The conference was sponsored by the *Société Saint-Jean Baptiste*, which comprised 250,000 to 300,000 members. Already in October, it had publicly declared that it stood for Quebec's political independence.[9] The conference was attended by about two thousand French Canadians from across Canada. Its purpose was to discuss the political future of French Canadians. It passed sweeping resolutions, which included independence as well as a list of powers for Quebec that filled eight lines of *Le Devoir*. These received a 90 percent approval from Quebec delegates. French-Canadian attendants from outside Quebec were dismayed by the turn of events and voted against most of the resolutions.[10] Quebecers seemed to be speaking with one voice. Even "federalist" Jean Lesage now condemned Trudeau's intransigence, declared his belief in a two-nations Canada, and held out an olive branch to his fierce opponent, Daniel Johnson, in order to fight Trudeau.[11]

In Quebec's legislature, unanimity did indeed reign supreme: a poll conducted by the *Toronto Daily Star* and *Le Soleil*, published on October 7, 1967, showed that 83.3 percent of its members favoured some sort of new constitutional arrangement. While slightly less than a third wanted some form of associate statehood, a third favoured political independence. Only a measly 2.6 percent defended the status quo.

Of course, Johnson could count on further support from France. Back in Paris after his "Vive le Québec libre!" speech, De Gaulle continued his meddling in Canadian affairs. While the Canadian premiers were meeting in Toronto, De Gaulle declared before a thousand journalists in Paris that there was a need for "a complete restructuring of the Canadian federation, which is governed today by an act decreed by the Queen of England a hundred years ago. In my opinion, this will inevitably lead to the sovereign state of Quebec, master of its destiny.... It is hard to envisage a different outcome."[12] De Gaulle was sure that the co-operation of France and Quebec would give a strong impulse to all French Canadians, including those living outside Quebec, in particular to Acadians whose attachment "to France, its language, and its soul," he found "émouvante" (touching).

A *Le Devoir* editorial tried to downplay De Gaulle's words, but not to rebuke them. The general had correctly described Quebec's grievances, Paul Sauriol wrote, but he was not promoting outright independence, since his plans included French Canadians outside Quebec. In other words, to paraphrase Sauriol, De Gaulle was promoting a sort of "souveraineté-association,"[13] or Johnson's "Canada à deux."

The Johnson-Trudeau Showdown

Johnson's path to victory seemed quite smooth ... except for one hurdle: Pierre Trudeau. But what could one man do against such a tide of support for Johnson's position? Trudeau had but few allies, but among them was

Marc Lalonde, Trudeau's friend and collaborator since the *Cité libre* days. They developed a closer relationship in Ottawa. When later Trudeau became prime minister, Lalonde became one of his most-trusted ministers — if not *the* most-trusted, especially for all matters pertaining to Quebec.

Lalonde wanted Trudeau's message to be heard as widely as possible. He managed to get his friend invited to deliver the keynote speech to the annual meeting of the Canadian Bar Association on September 4, 1967, but Trudeau's tough stance on the Constitution didn't go over very well. Liberal MPs started to wonder how they would "crawl out of the political dead-end" in which Trudeau's "constitutional rigidity" had trapped them.[14] The next day, in an interview with journalists, Trudeau summarily dismissed the "two-nation" approach, calling it an "intellectual hoax" — not the best response to endear him to nationalist Quebec reporters, who poked him harder and harder. Trudeau got more combative and called special status "une connerie" (BS) and "une grande fumisterie intellectuelle" (a big intellectual hoax). Most nationalists were outraged. Claude Ryan denounced "the deplorable attitude of Mr. Pierre-Elliott Trudeau" in his *Le Devoir* editorial of September 8. Focusing on his arrogance, he wrote: "Déplorable sur le plan intellectuel, l'attitude de M. Trudeau l'est tout autant sur le plan politique" (Deplorable on an intellectual level, Mr. Trudeau's attitude is just as deplorable on a political level). Trudeau seemed to be standing alone. Even Pearson started to waver, expressing his concern about the divisions in the party over Quebec.

Trudeau didn't seem very upset by his lack of support. On the contrary, he looked forward to the showdown that he knew would come at the federal-provincial conference in February 1968. Pearson had mandated him to produce the federal position paper. By the end of the year, *Federalism for the Future* was ready. This document, Trudeau's brainchild, was adopted by the federal government as its statement of policy to be presented at the February 5–7 constitutional conference. Right from the start, and contrary to what had become conventional wisdom in Quebec, Trudeau did not consider the 1867 Constitution to be a catastrophe. No, it was basically sound. In the context of the time, the founders of the BNA Act had done a good job; their "accomplishment was an act of great statesmanship."[15]

But it wasn't perfect. Trudeau identified two major flaws. First, "the people of French language and culture do not have the same opportunities as do those of the English language to live their lives ... or to realize their own potential ... in their own language in all parts of Canada."[16] Second, it was clear that nothing much had been done in the last hundred years "to make equality of economic and cultural opportunity as real and as meaningful for Canadians of French origin as it is for English-speaking Canadians." Trudeau warned that "the consequences of not doing so now could be serious."[17]

He identified the same inequality among regions. This is why the government of Canada hoped that this Conference "should mark the beginning of a process of constitutional review that will ... make equality of opportunity ... open to all Canadians, whatever their language or cultural heritage, and wherever they may choose to live or move."[18] Fortunately, affirmed Trudeau, it was not necessary to draft a new Constitution to correct these shortcomings. For example, of the many recommendations of the Royal Commission on Bilingualism and Biculturalism, "only two of these involve constitutional change and in no single case does the substance of action have to wait upon a change in the Constitution."[19] As for those changes that require a constitutional amendment, priorities had to be established.

The first priority "should be given to that part of the Constitution which should deal with the rights of the individual — both his rights as a citizen of a democratic federal state and his rights as a member of a linguistic community in which he has chosen to live. We [the government] propose the incorporation into Canada's Constitution of a Charter of Human Rights as quickly as the federal and provincial governments and legislative bodies can agree."[20] First, then, on the agenda: the rights of all Canadians.

The second item was to deal with the unequal opportunities between French and English Canadians. If "Canadian unity is to be preserved," then Canadians must urgently adopt the recommendations of the Royal Commission on Bilingualism and Biculturalism. For this purpose, "the Government of Canada ... proposes to recommend to Parliament, at its next Session, an Official Languages Bill that will formally declare English and French to be 'the official languages of the Parliament of Canada, of the federal courts, of the federal government, and of the federal administration.'"[21] Note that the recommendation was *not* that all Canadians should be bilingual, nor that all provincial governments should provide services in both languages. Only federal institutions that must represent both English and French Canadians had this obligation.

We don't know if the premiers fell off their chairs when they read the order of priorities established by the government for the conference, but we know that they didn't like it one bit: First individual rights? Then language rights? What happened to the revamping of the Constitution? Or to Quebec's demands for recognition? Or to a better distribution of powers between the federal and provincial governments, the main topic the premiers had discussed in their November meeting?

Further down, the federal document tried to allay their fears. It assured them that by agreeing to place these two issues as first priorities on the agenda, the federal government had in no way "overlooked the critical importance of determining which of the functions of government should be assigned to the two orders of government in Canada. Rather [it has] proclaimed [the] belief that the rights of people must precede the rights of governments."[22]

Having dealt with human rights and language rights, Trudeau could now set out his conception of Canada in the section appropriately entitled "The Nature of the Canadian Federation." It quickly became evident that Trudeau's view — the official government's view of Canada and its Constitution — was diametrically opposed to the one presented by Johnson in *Égalité ou indépendance*. Trudeau asserted that "Canadians are a free people in a free society." (In other words, Quebecers, like all Canadians, don't need to free themselves from any "colonizer.") As for the two-nation concept of Canada, he dismissed it in no uncertain terms: "Canada is a country of two founding linguistic communities, enriched by many heritages, and characterized by several regional identities.... Canada's identity is its diversity and its unity ... [flourishing] only as these communities and heritages and regions flourish. Canada is greater than the sum of its parts.... Only a narrow or static view of our country and of the world would lead one to believe that Canada can develop by the process of subtraction."[23]

Bang! The government — in the words of its Justice Minister Trudeau — was bluntly telling Johnson, his followers, and all other separatists that their grand project of independence was nothing more than a "process of subtraction," favoured by people with "a narrow or static view of our country and of the world." Whatever happened to Pearson's conciliatory government?

Regarding the division of powers, the Government of Canada assured premiers that these discussions would take place, but only "after the constitutional conferences have considered the other principal elements of the Constitution."[24] Unsurprisingly, Johnson's disapproval of this proposal was immediate: "Mr. Trudeau is apparently putting the cart before the horse."[25] In this response, he spoke for the collectivity of the premiers at their recent Confederation of Tomorrow Conference in Toronto.

De Gaulle Shenanigans Again: The Gabon Affair

The federal-provincial constitutional conference took place at a particularly tense moment in the relations between Ottawa and Quebec. According to Pierre Godin, Johnson's biographer, "Quebec–Ottawa relationships have never been so poisonous."[26] The cause? Gabon. Gabon? What did this little faraway African country, with a population of roughly two million people, have to do with a Canadian unity crisis? The culprit, in fact, was France, or more exactly De Gaulle. Gabon was a former French colony that had obtained its independence in 1960, but it was still quite dependent on aid, which France provided. Consequently, Gabon took advice from Paris very seriously.

In the fall of 1967, Gabon had invited Jean-Guy Cardinal, the Quebec minister of education, to a meeting to be held on February 6, 1968, in Libreville, its capital. All other ministers of education in attendance were members of sovereign states constituting the *francophonie*. Quebec alone was invited, not Canada, nor any other Canadian province. On matters of foreign policy, however, only the federal government had the authority to sign international agreements on behalf of Canada. France had already started to develop closer ties with Quebec under Premier Lesage. Now Quebec wanted to manifest its presence on the international scene. Both France and Quebec were trying to find ways to circumvent these restrictions, by positing that Quebec had the right to join the *francophonie*.[27]

The federal government protested. Always ready for conciliation, Pearson wrote to Johnson to suggest that Quebec could accompany the Canadian delegation to Gabon. Johnson didn't even bother to reply.[28] Quebec was thumbing its nose at Ottawa. According to Godin, "la guerre du Gabon" explained Johnson's conciliatory attitude at the premiers' conference: "If Johnson appeared to be so amenable in Toronto, it is because he is preparing, in collusion with Paris, a major confrontation with the federal government about the international role of Quebec.... Johnson is planning a no-holds-barred attack on the overseas front, in order to consolidate his domestic policy."[29] The Quebec delegation attended the meeting and was granted full state honours. In retaliation, Pearson officially broke off relations with Gabon, though everyone knew that France was the real culprit.

The Legendary 1968 Conference

February 5 arrived. Pearson welcomed all participants, including Johnson, in his usual affable way. He showed no sign of his displeasure — or anger — at the fact that on the same day, in faraway Gabon, the Quebec flag was flapping in the Libreville wind. As for Daniel Johnson, he didn't look or behave like a man who would break up Canada, according to journalist Peter Newman.[30] His image was relaxed, soft-spoken, and courteous, always appearing ready for compromise.

In his opening statement, Robarts, premier of Ontario, reminded everyone: "We are in the midst of a very serious crisis.... It is a crisis of the utmost gravity for our country because ... it is a crisis with respect to "our national will to survive." This, of course, was music to Johnson's ears. When his turn to speak arrived, he immediately confirmed that the crisis was real and the cause was obvious: the Constitution. It depicts Canada as a country made up of ten provinces, a "Canada à dix," whereas it really is a "Canada à deux," a Canada of two equal partners. The solution is simple, he told the participants: "Let us sit down together and write a new constitution."[31] He reassured everyone that he wasn't advocating a revolution. It was "not at all necessary to destroy *le Canada à dix* to create *le Canada à deux* ... but it has become absolutely essential and urgent to create *le Canada à deux* if we are to maintain *le Canada à dix*." To give some punch to the urgency of his request, he reminded all participants "that time does not work in favour of the Canada we have today."[32] Pearson reacted in his usual diplomatic way. He humorously admitted that he had difficulty understanding how "unlike the laws of mathematics, ten plus one equals two!"[33]

What would the recognition of this new nation entail, according to Johnson? Additional powers, of course. French culture was imperilled and had to be protected. He insisted that "if we [Quebecers] are to avert death by asphyxiation ... we must be present in certain areas, including those related to education, even in international relations." To add some pressure to his request, he added: "I do not want to sound alarmist, but we have several political parties in Quebec. There is the RIN, the RN and Mr. Lévesque's movement.... There is unanimity in Quebec with regard to these minimum requirements."[34]

Trudeau thanked Johnson for his presentation but said he needed some clarification on the notion of equality. If achieving equality meant giving increased rights to the French language throughout the country, the two were in total agreement. But Mr. Johnson seemed also to demand to extend the jurisdiction of Quebec, which he considered the homeland of the French-Canadian nation.[35] And there lay the problem: if Premier Johnson was demanding increased powers with regard to radio and television because the English-speaking majority was capable of threatening the survival of the French-speaking culture, why stop there? If the Quebec government could not trust the federal government for these matters, why not extend the same logic to banking, tariffs, international law ... and to every sector that comes under Section 91 of the Constitution? "How far will the demands of Quebec go? As far as the destruction of federalism?"[36]

When the Newfoundland premier's turn to speak came, "Joey" Smallwood wondered what would become of Quebec representatives in the federal Parliament. Would they be reduced to the role of "dummies if Quebec acquired the power of a nation-state?" He assured Johnson and the other participants that he had tried hard to understand Quebec's proposals: "Really I have! And I have failed.... Maybe because I am stupid. How anyone who loves Canada can advocate anything that would make Parliament impotent in order to make his own province strong baffles me, Mr. Prime Minister. I don't think any Canadian wants that."[37]

Trudeau was happy to repeat Smallwood's question: "Are the Quebec Members of Parliament nonentities?"[38] Indeed, he added, if "a federal minister from Quebec is not allowed to represent [his Quebec constituents] when it comes to external affairs, or radio and television, or all social matters, or economic institutions ... the consequence would be obvious. No politician worth his salt would want to come to Ottawa; he would want to go to Quebec where the decisions on these matters are taken."[39] Moreover, Trudeau continued, when one province is given "special rights" not granted to the other provinces, "not only would we be destroying the very reason for a French-Canadian presence in Ottawa,"[40] but we would clearly indicate that we no longer "have faith in federalism."[41] For him, speaking on behalf of the federal government, equality meant guaranteed equal language rights, and not special powers. French Canadians did not seek nor need them.

Furthermore, Quebec's request for more powers, he argued, was not a demand for equality, but for special privileges — or inequality. Trudeau went on to challenge the notion that Quebec constituted one nation. Even if one took the word "nation" in a sociological sense, he hypothesized, one would have to recognize that Quebec comprises not one but two nations, since "twenty percent of the population of Quebec is English speaking.... What does 'two nations' in Quebec mean?" he asked. "Must [this minority] also have certain political institutions?" To which he gave his own reply: "I think that to put the problem is to answer it."[42]

Johnson, visibly upset, shifted his attacks from the message to the messenger: "Mr. Chairman, I do not want to take undue advantage of your good nature, but I have just discovered that I might have more difficulty with the federal government's spokesman than with several of those representing provincial governments." As for Trudeau's message, he warned everyone that "it would be a serious error to believe that Quebec will be content once people elsewhere are able to speak French. I am sorry, but I must repeat what I said in Toronto. This problem cannot be solved with an aspirin tablet."[43] The whole federal system needed to be re-examined and renegotiated. It was this, he warned them, or else ... because "eventually, it will come to this: If the French-Canadian nation does not feel at home in confederation, there will be no more talk of a 'French Canadian nation,' but rather of a 'Quebec nation.'"[44]

The tension in the room was palpable. Pearson tried to dispel Johnson's concerns about the order of priorities set in the agenda. He assured him that if linguistic and cultural rights were put on the agenda first, it was not because they considered them to be the only or the major problems in any constitutional change. The government just thought that "it was not unreasonable to begin with basic fundamental rights that should go into a constitution." He agreed with Johnson that there was "a constitutional problem affecting the future of this country which was deeper than we put on item 2 [of the agenda]."[45]

Trudeau, for his part, was in no mood for conciliation. Going back to Johnson's remark, he declared: "I am a French Canadian and I am from Quebec, and the difficulty I see is not with the federal government, it is with federalism."[46] The gloves were off. Johnson interjected: "May I too make a correction, and I will make it in English because it is meant for my fellow premiers. When I talked about difficulties with the interlocutor, I did not mean the federal government specifically; it was with the Minister of Justice."[47] This ad hominem attack was too much, even for accommodating Pearson. He had to set the record straight: "The Minister of Justice," he retorted, "is a member of the federal cabinet. And in this government, of course, we adopt the principle, without qualification, of cabinet solidarity."[48] There was too much electricity in the air. Ever the diplomat, Pearson announced that it was his feeling that they should have a coffee break. When they returned, more barbs were exchanged, as claws were sharpened. Johnson tried to downgrade Trudeau by referring to him not as the minister of justice but as the deputy for Mount Royal. Unfazed, Trudeau retaliated, referring to Johnson not as the premier of Quebec but as the deputy for Bagot.

This extraordinary duel was being fought not only before the provincial premiers but in front of millions of Canadians, from coast to coast to coast, who could now, and for the first time, watch the federal-provincial conference live on television. They couldn't believe their eyes or their ears. On February 7, the *Globe and Mail* published an article aptly entitled "The Match of Johnson vs Trudeau." It reported that "in a 90-minute duel that starkly defined the gap between the federal government and

Quebec on the constitution ... provincial leaders watched, in evident fascination, the two Quebeckers trading subtle insults in a sparkling debate in which they staked out the positions they will occupy in the ongoing crucial negotiations."

There is no doubt as to who came out the winner. "Daniel Johnson has lost," Godin acknowledged. "It's a historical moment for the federalists who, since Lesage, have acquired the habit to be stripped [naked] by the provinces."[49] Trudeau's proposal for equal rights for French and English languages was approved by everyone except W.A.C. Bennett, premier of British Columbia. Trudeau's idea of integrating a Charter of Rights in the Constitution met with some resistance from Bennett, from Alberta's Premier Manning, and from Premier Robarts of Ontario, but his view of One Canada had clearly prevailed.

Johnson's scaremongering hadn't frightened anyone. His *Canada à deux* had found no supporter. In "Le duel Johnson-Trudeau," Claude Ryan underlined some deplorable aspects of the fight between the two, but he unequivocally sided with Johnson. He summarized the latter's demands: "Quebec wants complete or shared powers in three most urgent domains ... which are: social security, international relations, and radio-television. Furthermore, Quebec wants to proceed to a revision of jurisdictions in other domains such as: marriage and divorce, immigration, cinema, incorporation of companies, road transportation, professional relationships." He found nothing wrong in Johnson's position: "Truth be told, I see nothing in these demands that should be discarded a priori because they look too heretical from the perspective of a healthy federalist philosophy." For Ryan, it was Trudeau's rigidity and his blindness to what all Quebecers considered obvious that caused the fight.[50]

As for René Lévesque, he declared, unsurprisingly: "The federal-provincial conference has provided a blatant demonstration of the necessity of a sovereign Quebec. Except for those who hold stubborn illusions or fear any change ... this should be crystal clear." Dismissing Daniel Johnson's ambiguous stance, Lévesque said he didn't know if it stemmed from the premier's incapacity to express Quebec's aspirations and basic needs or from his "brilliant aptitude for indecision."[51]

Johnson went home empty-handed … and utterly crushed. According to Godin, he had been caught "entre les griffes de Trudeau" (between Trudeau's claws). When Johnson died, Marcel Cadieux, undersecretary of state and a friend since their university years, expressed his sadness, observing that Johnson's career in politics had been very successful … until Trudeau burst onto the scene. He truly believed that this had hastened his death.[52] So did Godin. It may well be true, although we know that Johnson had a heart condition. To his last breath, Johnson thought he would get even with his arch-enemy.

In late January, when rumours had it that Trudeau might participate in the race for the leadership of the Liberal Party, Johnson tried to undermine his prospects to succeed Pearson. During the conference, he warned reporters whom he met in the hallway that if Trudeau succeeded Pearson, "this would be enough to blow up Canada."[53] Overhearing it, Trudeau told them: "If Mr. Johnson's policies are followed, they will destroy Canada." During the race, Johnson pointedly let it be known that he had "no problem working with any of them except for one."[54]

When Trudeau won the leadership race for the Liberal Party, Premier Johnson worked heart and soul to prevent the Liberals from gaining power. He closely supervised the federal campaign, and, for a while, put the whole of the electoral funds and apparatus of the Union Nationale at the service of Stanfield's Conservative Party. Mocking Trudeau, he once called him "Lord Elliott," an allusion to Lord Durham. Every French Canadian would have learned at school that the much-hated Lord Durham had proposed in his 1939 *Report on the Affairs of British North America* the assimilation of French Canadians because they were "a people with no literature and no history." Trudeau responded tit for tat: "Calling me Lord Elliott when his name is Johnson is a sticky wicket." He added: Johnson's "comparison of me to Lord Durham shows how little he knows about history.… Durham didn't reach the same conclusions we did about linguistic rights. We're saying French Canadians should have these rights across Canada."[55]

Why was Johnson so viscerally opposed to Trudeau? There was certainly an element of personal vendetta, but he was also convinced that electing Trudeau would be "a national catastrophe. If Trudeau, Marchand and

Pelletier grab the levers of the federal government [he told anyone who cared to listen], it will be a bulldozer. Ten years of Trudeau, and it is game over. It will be the triumph of *One Canada*."[56]

Johnson died on September 26, 1968, exactly three months and one day after Pierre Trudeau's Liberal Party won a majority government.

THREE

Three Years a Liberal: Presto! Prime Minister

WHAT ARE THE CHANCES THAT A NEWLY MINTED LIBERAL, JUST THREE YEARS A MEMBER and bitter former critic of the party, would become the party's leader? And then the country's prime minister? What are the odds on that? Yet in short order, Pierre Trudeau made that transition. He had waited, taken his time to decide whether to become a candidate for the party leadership. Still, his candidacy seemed preposterous, a mockery, even he confessed, a huge practical joke played on himself and the party.

He threw his hat in the ring on February 16, 1968, a mere eighteen days before the official Liberal leadership election opened on April 6. This too had the makings of a joke. Such apparent nonchalance! Was Trudeau tempting fate, or silently yielding to it? Was this late entry too clever by half? Many thought so. Looking back in the rearview mirror of history, a flock of his biographers saw him *playacting*, delaying his announcement for dramatic effect and maximum advantage. Now, they thought, the "last in" had become a brilliant winning strategy. Too bad the other candidates hadn't figured this out.

Just Thirty-Three Days to Decide

Pelletier claimed that when Trudeau joined him and Jean Marchand for lunch at the Café Martin on January 16, 1968, Trudeau learned for the first time that it was he, not Marchand, who should run for the party leadership. Stunned by this news, Trudeau was said to have left his *boeuf bourguignon* untouched.

John English, Trudeau's official biographer, dismissed this story. Feigned surprise was just a coy ruse on Trudeau's part, English argued, since Trudeau knew of Marchand's reluctance to run. He also knew that Marc Lalonde had, during the Christmas holidays, set up a campaign office and program for Trudeau's candidacy. English suggested that this was all part of a deliberate plan to delay Trudeau's candidacy for maximum advantage. This interpretation was taken up by a host of Trudeau biographers, claiming Trudeau was just "playing hard to get."[1]

The possibility that Trudeau had good reason to be "stunned," or that he made his official declaration on February 16 because this is when he had made up his mind and felt ready to throw himself into the ring, isn't considered by these authors. In a book, also entitled *Trudeaumania* — like Litt's — Robert Wright rejected the notion of a conniving Trudeau, manipulating the media for the purpose of winning the leadership race. In fact, he devoted his whole book to dispelling such myths. He found no evidence for Trudeau's cunning nor any ulterior motives for not declaring his candidacy. Neither did we.

In fact, English provided a good reason for Trudeau's genuine hesitation but didn't give it the weight it actually deserved. He wrote that Trudeau wouldn't even consider being a candidate unless Marchand was not interested in the leadership and that he really wanted to make sure that Marchand's refusal was final.[2] Trudeau recalled, in his *Memoirs*, that Marchand was the obvious successor. Furthermore, even astute observers of the political scene could not see Trudeau as a potential candidate. He didn't even appear in the list of probable candidates identified by *La Presse*. Blair Fraser, who wrote on national politics in *Maclean's*, mentioned Eric Kierans as a possibility because he was bilingual, progressive, and anti-separatist, but he didn't even mention Trudeau, who had the same attributes and whom he had known since the 1950s. Dalton Camp included Trudeau in the list of *The Star Weekly* magazine of January 6, 1968, but rated him a long shot at 75–1, noting that as a "socialist and political dilettante," he was "just too much for the square majority of the Liberal party."

The only publication to consider Trudeau as a possible candidate was *Le Droit*, in the December 21, 1967, issue.[3] Obviously then, as late as January 1968, if, as the myth goes, rumours and talks about Trudeau's candidacy had been circulating for months, the media didn't seem to have noticed. Neither did Trudeau. If he had eyed the leadership of the party, would he have embarked on that minefield of reforming laws over divorce, homosexuality, and abortion?

The process leading to Trudeau's decision to run is very well described in George Radwanski's *Trudeau*, published in 1978. It has somehow disappeared from most of the regularly quoted sources. In it, Lalonde described in detail Trudeau's reasons for hesitating to become a candidate. It wasn't a lack of self-assurance: Trudeau never struck him as a guy who had misgivings about his ability to do the job. But it was simply too soon. He hadn't been around long enough. To go ahead, he needed to establish "whether he really had a serious chance to win." He feared that his run for the leadership could end in an ignominious defeat, destroying his credibility. As he confided one day to Marchand: "In Quebec, wouldn't I be a catastrophe?"[4]

True, Trudeau had by then a notable academic reputation. A collection of his previous essays was published under the title *Le fédéralisme et la société canadienne-française*. The French version turned out to be much more popular than anticipated. It made waves even in English-speaking Canada. The historian Ramsay Cook, who shared Trudeau's views on separatism, knew that an English translation would make him better-known across the country. He managed to convince Macmillan of Canada to publish the book. *Federalism and the French Canadians* came out in early January 1968 and quickly became a bestseller. The French and English versions sold nearly fifty thousand copies. As remarkable as this was by Canadian standards, it was surpassed by René Lévesque's *Option Québec*, which sold fifty thousand in the first three weeks following its release in 1968.[5] The two giants' relentless battle for the hearts and souls of French-speaking Quebecers was about to gain momentum.

When Pearson announced his retirement, Lalonde started to work behind the scenes to ensure that Trudeau would run. As for Trudeau, true to form, immediately after Parliament adjourned, he took off to a faraway land, this time Tahiti, for a Christmas vacation. Apparently, he was lured by a Club Med ad offering all-inclusive Tahiti for $599.95.[6] Lalonde recalled that "he left us with no indication that he was interested at all."[7] There Trudeau met the beautiful nineteen-year-old "flower child," Margaret Sinclair.

Would Trudeau Run?

The day he got back, jet-lagged, and probably still thinking about his chance encounter, he had dinner with Pelletier and Marchand. That's when Marchand firmly assured him that he was not running and pressured him to take it on. This is also when he learned that Lalonde had forsaken his holidays to work on a petition in support of Trudeau's candidacy, signed by more than six hundred writers, artists, academics, and journalists across the country. Is it surprising that he was "stunned" and left his *boeuf bourguignon* untouched? However, now that his trusted friends had planted a bug in his ear, he examined the possibility very seriously, weighing both his willingness to run and his chances of success.

Nationalists, of course, had labelled him *traître* (traitor) and *vendu* (sell-out) ever since he had gone to Ottawa. He also had another concern regarding Lalonde and Marchand. "If I go," he told them, "I want a commitment that you'll be around. I want to be sure you're not sending me out to war alone," especially as Gallup polls would show that, with him as leader, the Liberals would be trailing the Tories.[8]

He was probably impressed by the number of intellectuals, artists, and reporters who supported his candidacy, but was their support enough in the world of *realpolitik*? He wasn't the only one doubting its value. Frank Jones wrote in the *Toronto Star* that the people promoting Trudeau's candidacy were "the most ineffective bunch of political rooters a candidate ever had." Not only did they usually vote for the NDP, but they weren't delegates to the Liberal convention. An endorsement from them might well be "the kiss of death to a Trudeau who has to convince delegates he is a practical politician and not just a woolly academic. Everything about the committee for Trudeau bespeaks the political amateur."[9] So, Trudeau had many good reasons to hesitate.

By the end of December, he knew that his very popular reform of the Criminal Code had ironically also given him much notoriety. In January (after he had ascertained that Marchand would not run), thanks to Lalonde's discreet workings, he had a further chance to test the waters. This is when he visited every provincial capital and met every premier to present the federal government position on the unity crisis. At every stop, the media praised his intellect and his honesty. The people saw a man who wasn't mouthing platitudes and who genuinely cared about the issues.

When Trudeau came back from his tour, one encounter had a decisive impact on his future, according to the well-known Canadian journalist and writer Peter Newman. "That moment arrived on January 28, 1968,"[10] at the convention of the Quebec wing of the Liberal Party of Canada, held in Montreal. In this city, hotbed of radical nationalism of every variety, Trudeau strongly defended federalism. Despite the federal branch of the Quebec Liberal Party being in favour of the "two-nations" policy and many in its caucus regarding him as aloof and arrogant, Trudeau coolly and rationally presented his analysis of the present crisis. Yes, he told them, French Canadians were right in demanding equality, but there were better ways to obtain it than those proposed by misguided Quebec intellectuals and politicians. A guarantee of language rights in the Constitution would make them equal not only in Quebec but everywhere in Canada, because all of Canada is their homeland. He emphasized the view that one shouldn't confuse the rights of French Canadians with the desires of a provincial government to build its own empire. At the end of his speech, the mesmerized delegates jumped to their feet, chanting: "Il a gagné ses épaulettes!" (roughly equivalent to "For he's a jolly good fellow!").

At that moment, Newman wrote: "Whatever doubts had existed among his followers about the willingness of Quebec delegates to support his leadership had vanished." Journalists were most impressed. One of them wrote that anyone present knew that they had witnessed some kind of wonder, that something big had happened. Indeed, it is most unusual for one single speech "to change everyone's minds and reverse a high-profile policy."[11] "Cheers for Stand Against 'Special Status'" and "Trudeau Wins Quebec Round," trumpeted *The Toronto Telegram* on January 29.[12]

Claude Ryan was not enthused. He noted in *Le Devoir* that two events had taken place that day. The first was that the Liberal delegates had collectively expressed "an unequivocal act of faith in the future of federalism in Canada." The second was "the dedication of the overriding influence of Trudeau's thoughts." In other words, Trudeau's ideas had undeniably prevailed. Ryan attributed Trudeau's success "to the vigorous mental rigor, the subtle power of seduction, and to the courage of this public intellectual whose style is most unusual." Trudeau, he admitted, was a remarkable communicator. But Ryan deplored the position adopted by the delegates under Trudeau's influence. In his view, it didn't consider the complexity of the Quebec situation nor reflect prevailing views in Quebec. He warned Trudeau that if he wanted to win the leadership of the Liberal Party, he should be less "coolly logical and rational."[13]

Trudeau's ally and long-time friend, Gérard Pelletier, was also somewhat critical. His remarks underline a profound difference between the two that has rarely been brought to light. Indeed, Pelletier and Trudeau never actually saw eye to eye on their attachment to Canada. To the end of his life, Pelletier, unlike Trudeau, remained a "cerebral" federalist and a Quebec "soft" nationalist. Pelletier confided in his diary that Trudeau had spoken well, but he criticized his tasteless jokes about France-Quebec relations: "I don't understand the lack of sensitivity he puts on this matter, nor his apparent lack of respect for others' feelings on the subject."[14] In his speech, angry over the Gabon incident, Trudeau had poked fun at France's interference in Canadian affairs. He sarcastically noted that, as France had had seventeen constitutions since the revolution, it felt well qualified to advise others on them. This had drawn big laughs.[15]

The Politics of "Joual"

On February 13, 1968, Trudeau slipped, providing some political fodder to his French-Canadian nationalist opponents. It happened in English, on CBC's *Under Attack*. He was answering questions from francophone students at Carleton University. At one point he told them: "I think French Canadians have been betrayed by their elite for one hundred years." Asked about the need to grant more powers to Quebec, he answered that before asking for more powers, Quebec should do a better job with the ones it already had. Education falls under provincial jurisdiction, he said, so

Quebec couldn't blame the federal government for the fact that "our French is lousy."

This drew a storm of protests from all quarters in Quebec, including from Quebec liberals and newspapers like *La Presse*, who were generally favourable to Trudeau. René Lévesque ridiculed his statement: Trudeau was telling hungry Quebecers that before they could beg for their food, they should speak the proper French used in his high-brow circles. One article after the other blamed Trudeau for having made his statement to an English audience only too eager to scorn Quebecers. Some separatist reporters played on the double meaning of "lousy" (very bad — *très mauvais*, and full of lice — *pouilleux*.) They translated "lousy French" as *un français pouilleux*, a further proof that Trudeau despised his people and their language.[16]

Trudeau's expression was very harsh indeed. But he wasn't the only one deploring the quality of the French spoken and written in Quebec. Nor was he the first. In 1960, a book entitled *Les Insolences du Frère Untel* made history. It sold one hundred thousand copies, at a time when ten thousand was considered a bestseller. In it, Frère Untel (roughly translated as "Brother So-and-So" — his real name turning out to be Jean-Paul Desbiens) was a teaching priest. He didn't mince his words when he decried the abominable state of the French spoken by his students. He was the one who popularized the term *joual* (careless pronunciation of the word *cheval*) to refer to a kind of language he considered "primitive." This triggered a raging battle between those who agreed with Frère Untel and those — almost all of them nationalists and separatists — who considered *joual* a source of pride. For example, in 1973, an editorial in *La Presse* flatly stated that "joual is … a tribal dialect that couldn't pretend to convey a real culture. It's a language closer to animals than humans." On the other hand, nationalist Michel Tremblay wrote that same year that "someone who is ashamed of joual is someone who is ashamed of his origins, of his race, of being Québécois." Trudeau was thus doubly at fault: first for rejecting the opinion of some prominent nationalists about *joual*, and secondly for having forgotten that dirty linen should be washed in private, among French-speaking Quebecers only.

Trudeau had an intimate knowledge of the language problem. "When I was around fourteen or fifteen," he confided to George Radwanski, "I suddenly realized that the words I was speaking weren't really the words that were written. And I said: 'Either I start reading something else, or I start speaking a bit more the way it's supposed to be done.'" His decision happened almost overnight. He added: "I remember being penalized for it, because when you're fifteen and you suddenly begin to say '*le gateau*' instead of '*le gaaaateau*' people begin poking fun at you. Not only in school, but in the neighbourhood, and even some of my relatives. 'Oh, look, he's putting on airs.'"[17] Trudeau didn't budge. To a trained ear, his French accent was unique. No wonder: it was self-taught, imagined into being.

Trudeau's Candidacy: A "Huge Practical Joke"?

A welcome reassurance came on February 15, 1968, when a "draft Trudeau" petition appeared in the Quebec media. It was signed by two hundred prominent French Canadians, including the renowned actor Jean-Louis Rioux. Trudeau announced his candidacy the next day. At the press conference, he told reporters that they were the ones who had promoted his candidacy as "a huge practical joke on the Liberal party." They were daring the party to choose someone like Trudeau. He then added: "The joke blew up in your face and in mine. You know, people took it seriously." And now, they were stuck with him. Radwanski wrote that most people "took [his statement] as just another example of his cool, self-deprecating humour."[18] In fact, it was an entirely serious statement of his view.

There is no question that the enthusiastic attention given by the press to Trudeau's campaign played a vital role in its success. There were eight other candidates vying for the position: Joe Greene, Paul Hellyer, Eric Kierans, Allan MacEachen, Paul Martin, Mitchell Sharp, John Turner, and Robert Winters, but it was Trudeau who got the lion's share of the press coverage in English Canada. In francophone Quebec, fascination with Trudeau was less obvious. At first glance, Pierre O'Neil and Louis Martin seemed to interpret public opinion correctly when they told him, in a television interview, that he had no support in Quebec. Unperturbed, Trudeau answered: "We should wait and see."[19]

His televised spat with Johnson at the constitutional conference, which turned him into a rising star in English-speaking Canada, did not help his cause in Quebec. Claude Ryan, the editor of *Le Devoir*, chastised him daily for his stubbornness and rigidity and never endorsed his candidacy. He first promoted Mitchell Sharp, and as candidates fell out of the race, Ryan would pick any one except Trudeau until finally, contrary to tradition in Quebec, he endorsed the unilingual Paul Hellyer. Two important members of the Liberal Party, Maurice Sauvé and Maurice Lamontagne, were against Trudeau; René Lévesque called Trudeau the new *roi nègre*, an "Uncle Tom" slur that André Laurendeau had once affixed to Maurice Duplessis. Jean-Luc Pépin and Jean Chrétien, two young bright francophone ministers, had given their support to Sharp. Even in English Canada, Trudeau had fierce opponents. Laurier Lapierre, co-host of the very popular TV show *This Hour Has Seven Days*, criticized Trudeau for his antinationalism and his refusal "to grasp the profound need we have for a new constitution."[20] Many Liberals were outraged by Trudeau's tough stance on Quebec. They lamented that on the vital question of national unity, Trudeau had been "grossly irresponsible."[21] Trudeau stuck to his position on Quebec nationalism. He stood alone among all the other candidates.

TV allowed Trudeau to be seen and heard directly, bypassing the media's interpretation of his ideas. By 1968, there was a television in 95 percent of Canadian homes, and very few channels were competing for the viewers' attention. For example, the Liberal convention for the leadership of the party was viewed by approximately 17 million Canadians. They all saw Trudeau speak movingly of the death of Martin Luther King Jr., assassinated on April 4, and then go on to declare his faith in the triumph of a politics of reason over passion, and "the protection of individual freedom against the collective tyranny, and a just distribution of the national wealth."[22] They saw the enthusiastic cheering of the delegates, with journalists standing up and joining in.

It may come as a surprise that Trudeau was not always good on television. Radwanski and Wright observed that he delivered some of his speeches in a dull tone; he was terrible at reading prepared texts.[23] On June 9, during the first-ever televised leaders' debate, Trudeau spoke in a flat monotone, citing details of one policy after the other. He was "stiff and humourless," noted historian Ramsay Cook, and the debate "a debacle."[24] "Nobody really won," wrote Peter Newman, "the clear loser was the audience."[25] Jean-Pierre Fournier wrote in *Le Devoir*: "To bear yesterday's debate from beginning to end, one must have nothing else to do or be forced to do it by his newspaper."[26] Asked what he thought of it, Trudeau answered that he found it pretty dull and wouldn't want to impose another one on the Canadian public.

Trudeau's live speeches were usually remarkable, but there were some notable failures. A telling example happened on June 20, just a few days before the federal election. Trudeau was giving his last speech in Toronto, home of his biggest support, to a crowd estimated at more than fifty thousand — making it the largest political rally in Canadian history. Columnist Peter Newman, an unfailing supporter of Trudeau, wrote in the *Toronto Star*: "Pierre Trudeau's mammoth rally in Toronto's Nathan Phillips Square yesterday would have been an unqualified triumph if the prime minister hadn't opened his mouth.... His speech was so pedestrian that if almost any other politician had made it, he would have been booed."[27] Was tiredness a factor? Maybe. Trudeau's best speeches were unscripted, when he spoke from the heart.

Some have claimed that Trudeau's success was because he "learned to play to the camera,"[28] that he "had been working on his television persona for years."[29] Historian Paul Rutherford attributed Trudeau's meteoric rise to his acting ability: "He was something of a showman.... He had an instinctive sense of drama and timing that most professional actors would envy. He knew how *to appear* charming or firm, how to be witty or sincere, how *to seem* humble or shy, whatever the occasion might demand."[30] Note the loaded words: *to appear* charming; witty or sincere, *to seem* humble or shy. Rutherford offered no proof that it was all a facade. There is no question that Trudeau could outperform his rivals. On any debate with Stanfield, for example, the Conservative leader was no match. In the *Toronto Star* of May 27, 1968, Roy Shield compared the performances of Stanfield and Trudeau on the televised program *The Way It Is*, watched by two million viewers. He concluded that Stanfield must have regretted having ever left Nova Scotia, whereas Trudeau's "sense of communication on camera is as close to total as it can get. Many actors spend a whole life trying to achieve this same kind of presence. Few make it."[31] Almost all articles of the time underline Trudeau's remarkable presence on television, his innate talent to communicate. They don't seem to have noticed any manipulation of the media.

The media guru of the time, Marshall McLuhan, wrote about Trudeau: "The story of Pierre Trudeau is the story of the Man in the Mask. That is why he came into his own with TV."[32] The fact that Trudeau always hid behind a mask has become conventional wisdom. It was not an opinion shared by most Canadians at the time. People appreciated his "total lack of political rhetoric or … the vocal tricks that get so tiresome in other candidates." In other words, they appreciated his authenticity. On February 17, a journalist with the *Toronto Star* wrote enthusiastically, "The viewer … is left with the impression that the man is talking straight, that he believes what he is saying."[33] Article after article at the time underlined the public's admiration for a new kind of politics: a politics of issues rather than partisanship, of intelligence rather than ideology.[34]

It was often said that Trudeau was, and remained, an enigma. Anthony Westell and Geoffrey Stevens wrote in the *Globe and Mail* on April 9, 1968, that the Liberal Party has "honored the elevation to the leadership of the Liberal Party and shortly to the office of prime minister one of the most unusual, unlikely, and unknown figures in Canadian political history.… Thirty months ago, Mr. Trudeau was not even a Liberal.… today, he is the most powerful man in Canada … but he remains an enigma." In *Journey to Power: The Story of a Canadian Election*, Donald Peacock also attributed the fascination with Trudeau partly to the media, and partly to the fact that he "seemed such an enigma."[35] Keith Spicer, broadcaster, and later Canada's first commissioner of official languages, was exasperated at the growing references to an "enigmatic" Trudeau. In his article entitled "Strange He Is, but He Is Not a Stranger," published in the *Globe and Mail* on April 23, 1968, he attributed the myth to the public's own shallowness: "The significant Trudeau — the thinker, activist and leader — has fought among us openly, and in widening arenas, for a generation. The people of Canada know more about their new leader at the outset of his mandate than they knew about any predecessor after years of office.… He has revealed himself, his hopes, ideas and ideals, with a compelling clarity."

Was Trudeaumania Too an Illusion?

Trudeau's journey to the top was not an easy ride. Robert Wright argues, quite convincingly, that while "Trudeaumania was sweeping the land in the days before the Liberal leadership convention, the phenomenon was invisible to pollsters." A late March CBC poll revealed that Trudeau had the support of 606 delegates out of 2,475.[36] Another poll, published by the Canadian Institute of Public Opinion on March 20, 1968, gave Canadians the ideal profile of a future prime minister. "Whereas people in Quebec favoured a French Canadian, the rest of the country would rather have an English Canadian. In all of Canada, they agreed that he should be under fifty, that a cautious person was far better than a daring one, and they favoured a person with a business background. They didn't care if he looked good on television."[37] Apart from being barely under fifty, Trudeau's profile didn't quite fit the bill.

Even Trudeau's leadership victory on April 6, 1968, was by no means a foregone conclusion; nor was it a landslide. Although his candidacy gained much momentum during the last days of the campaign, it took four ballots for him to emerge as the leader. Even after the third ballot, he would have been defeated had John Turner thrown his support behind Robert Winters. Trudeau's election was greeted with lukewarm to negative reactions in Quebec. Johnson congratulated him but went back on the attack a few days later. Lesage was non-committal: he was going to wait and see. He didn't wait long. On April 10, the *Globe and Mail* reported that Lesage was "deliberately moving away from Trudeau's position." He was working on a revision of the Constitution close to the special status position defended by Gérin-Lajoie. Lévesque ironized that "Trudeau was offering Quebecers a happy drowning in the English majority."[38] He also predicted that those who thought that Trudeau was a man of action were in for a big disappointment.[39]

The Troubled Times of the 1960s

Trudeau's rise to leader of the Liberal Party and prime minister took place in 1968. The year was marked by social and political upheavals in many countries in the Western world and is also regarded by many historians as the most explosive year in that troubled decade. Already, on November 22, 1963, the assassination of John F. Kennedy by Lee Harvey Oswald had shocked both the nation and the world. It was followed by years of race riots in major American cities, of violent counter-reaction by police and security forces, and of the disastrous war in Vietnam, with massive anti-war marches taking place in the U.S. and around the world.

On April 4, 1968, at the convention for the leadership, just as Pearson was delivering his goodbye speech to roughly nine thousand party faithful, word came that Martin Luther King Jr. had been gunned down in Memphis. Canadians were shocked. The media's attention shifted from the Liberal convention to the devastating news of the assassination. Clearly, the United States was in turmoil. Trudeau's campaign for the federal election unfolded in a climate of unprecedented unrest. University campuses in North America and Europe had to face students' defiance of authorities. In France, what started as student protests ended up in a quasi-revolution. Factory workers throughout France walked off the job, leading to a general strike that involved some ten million people, and paralyzed the country. President Charles de Gaulle tried to repress the strikes but was overwhelmed. He disappeared and secretly ensured the support of the army in case he needed to retake Paris from the revolutionaries. When he came back, he dissolved the National Assembly and called an election for the end of June.

On June 5, senator and presidential candidate Robert F. Kennedy was mortally shot in Los Angeles. That night, Trudeau gave a speech in Sudbury. He had just come back from Montreal, where, accompanied by Pelletier and Marchand, he had attended the journalist André Laurendeau's funeral. A crowd of nationalists had verbally attacked them, shouting "Traitors!" and "Go back to Ottawa!" Trudeau's nerves were on edge. Instead of reading the speech prepared for him by Ramsay Cook, he spoke extemporaneously, venting his emotions. He urged the crowd of six thousand to use reason over passion. He incited them not to "tolerate those who speak with a language of hate and violence to achieve what they think is justice for their ideas." Those people, he told them, were the FLQ and their bombings, but also the English-speaking hecklers he had encountered on his campaign trail who had shouted at him: "'Frenchman Go Home! Damn Communist,' or 'Bloody Fascist'.... This is not the kind of dialogue on which a civilization is built." The audience was captivated. Lester Pearson confided to Marc Lalonde that this was the finest political speech he had ever heard.[40]

And So Came the 1968 Election

On April 23, Trudeau announced at the House of Commons that he had requested the Governor General to dissolve Parliament. A general election would be held on June 25. The House simply adjourned, without a word of appreciation or farewell to Lester B. Pearson, who expressed his disappointment in his memoirs in his usual good-humoured way. He regretted that nobody had thanked him for his "incomparable services to Canada, to the world, to the interplanetary system."[41] When Trudeau was asked why he had not paid tribute to Pearson, he replied: "I would have liked to thank Mr. Pearson, former external affairs minister Paul Martin … and former solicitor-general Lawrence Pennell." But a statement of this sort would have entailed replies from opposition leaders; would have been out of place when he had in his pocket a proclamation declaring that the 27th Parliament no longer existed.[42] This may well be the case, but the incident remains regrettable. Much to his credit, Pearson didn't hold a grudge against Trudeau. He stood by him in many rallies. The editorial of the *Globe and Mail* of June 20 quoted Pearson's laudatory remarks: "I feel happy leaving the country and the Government of Canada in his hands. I think of him as a very wise, intelligent patriot. He has been loyal to the language, the culture and the traditions of Quebec but he has put above all of that his loyalty to Canada."

Why did Trudeau dissolve Parliament to hold elections in June, when it was generally assumed that they would be held in the fall? Trudeau's answer, as he told the *Toronto Star* on April 27, was that "this parliament has worn itself out.… It has not been a happy parliament." Others argue that political strategists had recommended to advance the date to take advantage of the surge of what came to be called Trudeaumania. It was completely astonishing for Trudeau, a middle-aged politician, to be mobbed by screaming teenage girls as if he were a rock star. The media played up his athletic flips in swimming pools, his canoeing through rapids, or his taking daring runs down ski slopes. The athleticism and youthful appeal were real, and they caused an unprecedented rise of interest and participation in politics. In 1968, "millions of Canadians have suddenly become fantastically interested in, of all things, Canadian politics," *Maclean's* reported. In Alberta, for example, only two Liberals had been elected since 1957. When the Liberals started to nominate candidates for the election, Liberal Party memberships were selling at the amazing rate of four hundred a day.[43]

Trudeau was not fooled by the sudden surge in interest. He knew it would fade quickly. On June 20, at the North York Centennial Centre, in Ontario, he urged the forty-thousand-strong cheering crowd to remain interested in politics after the election because this is how democracy is maintained. "We have a party to get you involved in politics," he told them. "If you don't like ours, get involved in another one. Our party will continue to operate after the election, paid for by Liberals like you, and we will come to you, not with more promises, but with a demand that you keep yours."[44]

Trudeau did not find much support in the Quebec media nor among its intellectuals and politicians. Throughout the campaign, much of the Quebec press was against him. Even the English *Montreal Gazette* and the *Sherbrooke Daily Record* proclaimed their support of the Tories. Predictably, *Le Devoir* endorsed Stanfield. Surprisingly, Johnson, who hated Trudeau with a passion and had put his weight behind Stanfield, announced on April 24 that he would remain neutral. Did he have a sudden change of heart? Not really. The pressure came from his own party. Trudeau's support among Quebecers, including French-speaking voters, was gaining a lot of momentum despite the Union Nationale's opposition. With an eye on the next provincial elections, pundits of the party felt that, with Trudeau's unstoppable surge in popularity, it was safer to keep a low profile in the federal elections. The next day, "federalist" Jean Lesage also announced that he would remain neutral.

Trudeau has always been a controversial figure, capable of eliciting adoration and hatred with almost equal intensity. The Trudeaumania phenomenon overshadowed a well-orchestrated smear campaign that spread widely alongside the kisses and love-ins. Both Litt and Wright devoted many pages to the details of these vicious attacks. In an article aptly entitled "The Facts and Fictions of the Trudeau's Smears," Peter Newman expressed his outrage. He wrote: "Never before in a Canadian election has a prime minister been the subject of so much hatred and innuendo as has been flung at Pierre Trudeau in the current campaign."[45] Trudeau was showered with of all sorts of accusations, from being a communist intent on turning Canada into a communist country like China, to being homosexual.

The omnibus bill of 1969 containing criminal law reforms had become a major issue in rural Quebec. The worst smear campaigns came from the Montreal-based Les Pélerins de Saint-Michel, a conservative group that had broken from Réal Caouette's Ralliement des Créditistes (a sort of Quebec branch of the Social Credit Party). In their publication, *Vers demain*, which claimed a circulation of ninety thousand, Louis Even, director-general of the organization, "identified Trudeau with international communism, anticlericalism, perversion and subversion." He asserted that it was "with the stench of Sodom that P.E. Trudeau presented himself for the leadership of the Liberal party." His "omnibus bill" legalizing homosexuality and permitting abortion clearly showed that Trudeau was "marked by the sign of the Beast." Louis Even hoped that Michael the Archangel would draw his sword "to protect people he loves against rottenness and the domination of Satan."[46] At first, some members of the Conservative Party were helping to spread these rumours, *sotto voce*. They linked Trudeau's reform bill on homosexuality with the mention that he was a bachelor. As the election drew near, these whispered accusations grew louder and louder.

In Toronto, Reverend Harold C. Slate, minister of Jarvis Street Baptist Church, and president of the Canadian Council of Evangelical Protestant Churches, firmly believed in a worldwide communist conspiracy. He published a translation of a pamphlet written by W.J. Ewin, a Baptist missionary in Quebec, which aimed at saving Canada from Trudeau's communist plot. The glossy booklet ran through three printings and sold almost twenty thousand copies.[47] The politics of smear had started even before the Liberal leadership race. Ron Gostick, head of the Canadian Intelligence Service, had published a "news sheet" accusing Trudeau of being a communist. His pamphlets had a great influence on the publishers of *Vers demain*. In late March, four thousand copies of a French-language booklet entitled *On a "fourré" la vieille garde* (The Old Guard Was Screwed) was mailed to every Liberal convention delegate in Ontario and Quebec, to all members of the Ontario and Quebec provincial legislatures, and to every national news outlet in Canada.[48]

At first, Trudeau brushed off these attacks, considering them unworthy of rebuttal. In June, however, with the approaching election, he finally addressed them publicly. "It's the first time that I've even bothered to mention them in this campaign," he told his supporters in P.E.I. Although it was well known that members of the Conservative Party were participating in spreading these vicious attacks, Trudeau hadn't accused them, "because," he said, "there are all kinds of sick people in our society." He urged politicians of all parties to dissociate themselves "from this kind of garbage."[49] In Quebec City, on June 15, Trudeau turned to more direct accusations. "There are publications like *Vers demain* which are being distributed by certain Conservative candidates. It doesn't disturb me if they attack me, but they are trying to exploit in the people hate, ignorance and envy." On June 20, both the Canadian Council of Churches and the Evangelical Fellowship of Canada came to Trudeau's defence and denounced these attacks. "Innuendos, sly suggestion, smut and smear should be unknown in the lexicon of the Christian," they declared.[50]

What were the issues that dominated the June 1968 election? According to John English, "no fundamental realignment and no great dividing issues characterized the election of 1968. Indeed, journalists struggled to find issues that separated the parties, especially in English Canada."[51] True, this election will not be remembered for the contestants' divergent options about economics, foreign policy, or regional disparity. But no other election seemed so crucial to voters or to speak so directly to the sheer survival of Canada. This matter set Trudeau apart from all others. He stood alone.

His outright rejection of a two-nation Canada or of any form of special status for Quebec drew sharp criticism from many quarters. As soon as he announced the election, Charles Taylor, his long-time friend, now an NDP candidate and party vice-president, declared that Trudeau's "magic aura won't resist very much hard concentration of the problems facing Canada.... What he's putting forward would be terrible for the country."[52] Two months later, Robert Cliche, Quebec NDP leader, agreed with Taylor that Trudeau was "the greatest obstacle to Canadian Unity."[53]

Remember the Gabon affair? In April, Quebec — and not Canada — was invited again to an education conference of the *francophonie*. But, by this time, Trudeau had been elected leader of the Liberal Party. He still insisted that only Ottawa was empowered to deal with international relations, and on May 8, he declared his willingness to make it an election issue. Johnson was quick to respond that Trudeau's rigidity was "a good way to raise prejudice and create turmoil in Canada."[54] While federal opposition parties agreed that international affairs were a federal responsibility, they nevertheless all blamed Trudeau for his inflexibility. Tommy Douglas, the NDP leader, affirmed that Trudeau's manoeuvre did nothing to promote unity.[55] Stanfield accused him of using tactics that divided Canada for partisan purposes. Matters such as these, he said, should be quietly negotiated in a federal-provincial constitutional conference. He expressed his deep concern that a feud between Trudeau and Johnson "could wreck future constitutional negotiations."[56]

Trudeau's answer was fast and clear: Stanfield was confusing the views of Marcel Faribault, his Quebec lieutenant, and of Premier Johnson with those of ordinary Quebecers. "This isn't Quebec," he retorted, "Quebec is ... Canadians of all origins, but mainly French, who believe that Canada is their land and their home, and they want their representatives in Ottawa to speak for Quebec in international affairs. Mr. Johnson is elected by Quebecers to speak for provincial affairs, not federal affairs and certainly not international affairs." He added that if people disagreed with the way he was responding to Johnson's actions, "they had better not vote for me."[57]

The Quebec Conservatives were delighted when Marcel Faribault agreed to become a Tory candidate. So was Ryan in *Le Devoir*. Remember that Faribault was behind the notion of "two founding peoples," translated in brackets as *deux nations*. Regrettably for the Conservatives, Stanfield and Faribault didn't quite see eye to eye on the unity question. Their different perspectives came back to haunt them during the campaign. Stanfield spoke of two peoples, but one Canada, Faribault of a two-nation Canada. Stanfield was skating around their differences, leaning over backward to please Quebec voters.

Trudeau was quick to criticize the ambiguity. When told that Stanfield had complained that he had distorted the Conservative position, he candidly replied that he couldn't have done it for the simple reason that he didn't know what their position was. "Perhaps the conservatives had better decide who is speaking for them.... The distressing thing is not the two-nation policy. It is the two-policy policy."[58] Trudeau rejected both Stanfield's and Faribault's theses. "If we accepted the thesis of Mr. Faribault et al.," he told a Winnipeg audience, "we should logically conclude that there are many nations in Canada: Italian, Jewish, Polish, Scottish, Irish."[59] He reiterated the same view at a rally in Markham, Ontario. He told the 5,000 people present, with 1,800 standing outside, many of whom were new Canadian participants, that the political two-nation concept would leave a "hell of a lot of them out."[60]

Some have attributed Trudeau's great success in English Canada to his categorical rejection of "special status" or of the two-nation policy. He was going "to put Quebec in its place." Trudeau was aware of the misconception. Sometimes he would skillfully turn the argument around: "Yes," he would say, "I want to put Quebec in its place, and its place is within Canada." Most of the time he would simply clarify his position. For example, on May 24, 1968, he gave a talk at the Canadian Club of Winnipeg. This is how Fernand Beauregard reported it in *La Presse*: "Mr. Trudeau declared that he agreed with Quebec's legitimate aspirations.... He warned all those who imagined that he was going to become the self-appointed champion of English Canadians' opposition to Quebec's aspirations... to vote for another candidate on June 25."[61] A month later, he took the same stand in Alberta: "We are not waging this campaign against Quebec. If anyone wants to vote for our party because they think we will put Quebec in its place, they shouldn't, because that is not my intention."[62]

Trudeau did not shy away from taking unpopular positions during his campaign. For example, at a rally in Southern Ontario, he told his supporters: "No government is a Santa Claus.... We don't intend raising taxes any more than we have to and, therefore, we aren't making any promises in this election."[63] In Brantford, he reiterated the same message. "Well, we're not going around telling people that the government will give them more, and give great public works here, and build a tunnel there, and increase all benefits in the next place. We are saying that the revolution of rising expectations can be a danger to Canada if the people think that governments have money of their own and they can give things away that don't cost the people anything."[64] Conservative Ontario farmers were very impressed by what they called "a straight shooter."

Trudeau wasn't always met by cheering crowds. More often than not, he was heckled by nationalists and separatists who came to his rallies in large numbers. He never hesitated to counterattack. He accused some of being afraid that the country was no longer interested in their small minds and small ideas.[65] On June 6, the day Senator Kennedy died, Trudeau was in Rouyn, in Northern Quebec. When young separatists heckled him, shouting, among other cries "Vive le Québec libre!" Trudeau lashed out angrily: "You can have your free Quebec but what about your freedom of speech?... There would be no freedom of speech in your *Québec libre*. You are conducting yourselves like tramps and you want to run the affairs of this province?... Senator Kennedy was killed by purveyors of hate like you!" the *Toronto Star* reported.[66] In the editorial of *Le Devoir*, Vincent Price had a slightly different take on the event. He condemned the hecklers, but he didn't like Trudeau's response: "He went too far in his rebuttal. He has exaggerated," he wrote. His attitude was "too bellicose. He could have used less sarcasm and more diplomacy."[67]

Prior to Kennedy's murder, Trudeau had been accompanied, and guarded, by two plainclothes RCMP officers. After that, the RCMP and the local police didn't take any chances. And for good reason. Not only was the world a more dangerous place, but the police confirmed that there were threats on Trudeau's life in almost every place he went. Tensions reached their peak on June 24, Saint-Jean-Baptiste Day.

On Election Eve: A Riotous Saint-Jean-Baptiste Day in Montreal

The first Saint-Jean-Baptiste Day parade took place in Montreal in 1843. It has since been celebrated every year, in every village, town, and city in Quebec, with Montreal and Quebec City holding the biggest parades. In 1977, René Lévesque renamed it "Fête nationale," politicizing it and eliminating its religious character. The celebration of 1968 was unlike any other in the way it unfolded and the way the press reported it. In the English media, the retelling has been consistent, give or take a few details. In the French, however, there have been two basic interpretations from the beginning. For most francophones, it is possible to determine the political leanings of the authors by the press title. Compare "Émeute de la Saint-Jean — Nuit de violence" (Saint-Jean Riots — Violent Night) to "Le lundi de la matraque" (Truncheon Monday).

Let us first look at the facts as we know them from various sources. The riotous and violent Saint-Jean "celebration" left in its aftermath 123 injured people — some very seriously — including 43 policemen, and 292 arrests, including Pierre Bourgault, leader of the separatist RIN (Rassemblement pour l'indépendance du Québec). People witnessed police brutality, but they also saw demonstrators' aggressive conduct: setting fires, overturning police cars and scorching others. Pop bottles filled with various substances flew around, one reaching the VIP reviewing stand, which included Pierre Trudeau, Daniel Johnson, Jean Drapeau, and Archbishop Paul Grégoire. When another bottle flew past them, all beat a retreat except Trudeau, who refused to be drawn to safety by his bodyguards and who looked down defiantly upon the crowd. The next day, his party won a majority.

Quebecers were quickly split on who to hold responsible for the riot. Compare, for example, the editorials of *La Presse* and *Le Devoir* of June 25. In "Toute notre indignation" (Our Total Indignation), Roger Champoux, editor of *La Presse*, could hardly contain his anger and outrage: "The revolting tsunami of violence has reached Canada's metropolis. What could have been an exhilarating, pride inspiring celebration of our *Fête Nationale* has turned to a bloodbath.... In the name of the whole population we can't express enough our indignation." Champoux attributed the riots to "un groupe de fanatiques" (a group of zealots), to too many young people "who let themselves be drawn into the whirlpool of fanaticism." He concluded with the following cry: "The whole French-Canadian society is upset, worried, and shouts its indignation."

The tone of the editorial of *Le Devoir* of June 26 was quite different, and so was the message. Like Roger Champoux, Claude Ryan had harsh words for the separatist rioters: "They have profoundly discredited the cause they allegedly serve. They pretend that they love their people, but they behaved like human beings full of hate." But Ryan thought the police behaved no better, letting their hatred of separatists override their duty to preserve order. People witnessed "scenes of arrests unworthy of civilized policemen." Ryan recognized that "Trudeau showed undeniable courage by calmly remaining seated." However, the rioters' distaste of Trudeau was understandable: "The demonstrators hostile to Mr. Trudeau nurture a dislike of his ideas which is legitimate in a democracy." So, in this editor's twisting and turning, who does he blame for the riots? Ryan put the onus squarely on Trudeau: "Prime Minister Trudeau has committed a serious and regrettable mistake when he decided to attend the parade in spite of the difficulties of which everyone was aware." Granted, Trudeau showed courage, Ryan wrote, but it would have been better if he had shown "a better practical judgment by abstaining from going to the event." In other words, according to Ryan, the prime minister of Canada should have allowed some separatist hotheads to succeed in their scare tactics. So, Trudeau's attendance was somehow the real cause of the violence.

Pierre Bourgault — who turned out to be the instigator of the riots — must have rejoiced at this editorial. A few days before the parade, he had stated publicly that "June 24 is French Canadians' national day, not July 1st." Since Trudeau did not recognize the existence of the French-Canadian nation, "he had no business attending it and strutting about like a peacock."[68] This version of the Saint-Jean riots soon gained traction. For diehard nationalists, Trudeau became solely responsible for the protests. He came to the parade to show off, to provoke the French-Canadian "nation." Fifty years later, Jules Falardeau, son of Pierre Falardeau, the very well-known separatist filmmaker, made a documentary in which he expressed the identical view: "June 24, 1968, Pierre-Elliott Trudeau comes to taunt Quebecers by showing up at the dignitaries' platform during the celebration of Saint-Jean-Baptiste Day, whereas a few days before, he had denied their existence as a nation."[69] An ex-policeman by the name of Aubin recalled in an interview in the same video that Trudeau's mere presence was "shocking." His waving to the crowd was "arrogant."

Trudeau gave a different reason for his attendance. In his *Memoirs*, he recalled having been invited by Mayor Drapeau, who soon after advised him not to attend, because his presence "was likely to provoke separatist riots." Trudeau answered that he would attend, since he had already accepted the invitation: "I was certainly not about to admit, by chickening out, that the Prime Minister of Canada could not attend the Saint-Jean festivities in his native city! I had attended this parade since I was 6 years old."[70]

Excessive police brutality has been singled out in many documents, written or televised. Equal violence perpetrated by protesters is often forgotten or mentioned "en passant." Look up "le 24 juin 1968" on Google, and many entries for "Le lundi de la matraque" (Truncheon Monday) will appear. The separatist magazine *Parti pris* was the first to focus exclusively on police brutality in a book entitled *Le lundi de la matraque*. The authors, Jacques Lanctôt and Paul Rose, later to become convicted criminals in the kidnapping of British diplomat James Cross during the October Crisis of 1970, had been arrested and held in jail that night. They complained of police brutality, and again, fifty years later in the Fallardeau documentary, said that they "were [merely] protesting naively" and were met with a police brutality, almost on par with Chile's, under the dictator Augusto Pinochet. And so it goes: alternative narratives and witnesses for the night of June 24.

Election Day

The following day, Canadians chose their next government, granting the Liberals the majority that had eluded them since 1962. There is no question that Trudeau's courageous attitude during the parade contributed to the election results. But it was not by any means the sole reason for his success. Despite nationalist opposition, Trudeau was immensely popular in Quebec. The day of the riots, ten thousand people showed up at Liberal rallies in two contested ridings close to Montreal. On June 21, thirty-five thousand had come to hear him at Place Ville-Marie in Montreal. Trudeau's rejection of the two-nation policy was supposed to hurt the national feelings of all French Canadians. As it turned out, the Liberals secured fifty-five seats out of seventy-four, and the Liberal popular vote in Quebec rose by eight percentage points over the 1965 election.

Claude Ryan was not impressed. He did not take the results as an endorsement of Trudeau's political stance on Quebec nor of English Canadians' necessarily voting against Quebec's demands. Rather, they had found in Trudeau their saviour: "English Canada … has more likely opted to vote for its own security." As for Trudeau's great success in Quebec, he was sure that "the Quebec people haven't explicitly endorsed all the constitutional ideas of Mr. Trudeau." Many French Canadians just voted for one of their own. Ryan was still convinced that "national aspirations are at the heart of every French Canadian." He used his *Le Devoir* editorial of June 26 to make one more implicit attack on Trudeau: only the blind and inflexible attitude of one kind of nationalism can deny the existence of the other one.

La Presse sang a very different tune on June 26. The very titles of many articles speak volumes. The editorial "Un parti, un chef, une équipe" (One party, One Leader, One Team) rejoiced that the country had finally secured a majority government and hoped that the Liberals would implement some of the needed reforms. "The liberal party has led a fascinating, and exciting battle."

The opinion piece on the editorial page was even more enthusiastic. In "Le Québec a parlé clair" (Quebec Has Clearly Spoken), the journalist, and future senator, Renaude Lapointe, offered an interpretation of the Liberals' victory radically different from Claude Ryan's: "Yesterday, Quebecers gave an unequivocal mandate to Trudeau and his team. They gave them this mandate in spite of … the verbal terrorism, and the concrete terrorism aimed at the population by separatist groups of all shapes and sizes, and in spite of the heinous and obscurantist propaganda that has swept the province." She argued that Trudeau had won on two levels. First, he won over his political opponents, but mostly, "he triumphed over more ferocious adversaries: the antifederalist strongholds." She had a few kind words for the NDP. She deplored the fact that our electoral system penalizes third parties, and that the NDP was its principal victim. At each election, this party failed to gain the number of seats that reflected its share of the popular vote. As for the Conservatives, she wrote, they faced a humiliating defeat in Quebec. They had hoped to gain some twenty-two seats thanks to M. Marcel Faribault's candidacy and the Conservatives' new position on the Constitution. Instead, they ended up reducing their seats from eight to four. Faribault's ambiguous "two peoples/deux nations" concept didn't fly, not even in his own riding, where he lost his seat.

Trudeau interpreted his victory as an endorsement of his position on Canadian unity: "It is the victory of all those who believe in the future of Canada." But he warned everyone that neither the party nor the population could rest on their laurels. "I am not a magician," he reminded Canadians in his concluding remarks, "I said it, and repeated it all along the campaign. To shape our future, we'll need a lot of work, work guided by reason and brotherly love. I swear my commitment to it, and I invite all citizens to do the same."

FOUR

Trudeau Launches the Just Society

FORTUNE SMILED UPON PIERRE TRUDEAU, REWARDING HIS INITIATIVES AS JUSTICE MINister and his daring gamble to become prime minister. His crowning achievement thereafter was a new Liberal majority in Parliament after years of minority government. In a remarkably short time, he had even become a charismatic hero in the eyes of many Canadians. So far, politics wasn't turning out to be so hard a profession for him. Seizing the opportunity to lead, Trudeau felt confident that he could take his ideas forward and make of Canada a Just Society. As a first step, he thought, why not then bring justice to those most dispossessed and disadvantaged in the country, Canada's Indigenous Peoples?*

Just days in office, he began this surprising undertaking. Trudeau had not written or spoken much on Indigenous matters, nor had he made it a feature of his election campaign. His focus instead seemed always to be on Quebec separatism and Canadian national unity. Yet we should have known how appealing this file would be to a man with his liberal cast of mind, intent on bringing rights to "Indians," long set apart by racism. Typical of

* While the terminology has changed dramatically since the events described in this chapter, we use the term "Indigenous" throughout, except in citations or in direct reference to the language used and understood at the time.

Trudeau, this policy initiative would be bold and governed by first principles. Would political fortune yield this time to the charismatic actor? Would it give way to comprehensive reform on a subject of such enormous magnitude? That was the question.

Knowingly walking into a political minefield, as he would do many times during his political career, Trudeau went straight ahead. He knew a fundamental grappling with the "Indian Problem" would bring Indigenous Peoples into serious comprehensive dialogue with the Canadian people and governments. The virtue of the minefield then is that it would, one way or another, move the needle forward on this issue in a way that all prior more limited initiatives had not.

Let us hear Trudeau as he gave voice to the tragedy of Indigenous Peoples in Canada in a speech in Vancouver, August 8, 1969:

> We have set the Indians apart as a race. We've set them apart in our laws. We've set them apart in the ways the governments deal with them. They're not citizens of the province as the rest of us are. They are wards of the federal government.... They have been set apart in law ... and they've been set apart socially too.
>
> [So we are] at a crossroads — the time is now to decide whether the Indians will be a race apart in Canada or whether [they] will be Canadians of full status.[1]

The language here has a daring liberal ring, seemingly offering justice at last. Peoples set apart shall be freed, embraced enjoined. This liberal call for justice regarding Indigenous Peoples aimed at a Canada with *equal rights for all.* But was this conception of justice compatible with Indigenous understandings? Trudeau opened the door to debate the matter and invited Indigenous Peoples at this crossroads to choose their direction. The call would in due course be answered, and the whole course of Indigenous policy in Canada would be shaped by it.

Looking Backward, Looking Forward*

Trudeau was right. A backward glance on Indigenous Peoples in Canada showed them as a race apart both before and after Confederation. Treated as outcasts, they were not considered ready to live alongside other Canadians. Confined to their tribal systems on "lands reserved for Indians," the aim of Canadian policy was to set Indigenous Peoples apart until over time they would have gradually become assimilated and brought into conformity with the so-called superior white man's civilization. Canada's first prime minister, John A. Macdonald, spelled out the policy in 1887 very clearly:

> The great aim of our civilization has been to do away with the tribal system and assimilate the Indian people in all respects with the inhabitants of the Dominion, as speedily as they are fit for the change.[2]

Almost half a century later, the notion of "assimilation to a higher civilization" continued to be the governmental theme. In 1931, Duncan Campbell Scott, the deputy superintendent of the Department of Indian Affairs, claimed that the whole purpose of educating the "Indians" was to "enfranchise" them into being "real" Canadians:

> The Government will in time reach the end of its responsibility as the Indians progress into civilization and finally disappear as a separate and distinct people, not by race extinction but by gradual assimilation with their fellow citizens.[3]

Such was the ugly face of "Indian" policy in Canada: apartheid followed by assimilation. It bore the features of triumphant imperialism that rejected any notion of consulting the Indigenous Peoples, or even an attempt to know their own wishes. The premise in both cases was that "We," white

* We wish to acknowledge our deep indebtedness to the many scholars cited in this chapter whose work has so powerfully shaped our understanding and narrative on this subject. In that regard, we note especially the fine extensive research of Sally M. Weaver, *Making Canadian Indian Policy: The Hidden Agenda 1968–70* (Toronto: University of Toronto Press, 1981).

people, knew what "They," Indigenous Peoples, wanted or, rather, should want. "We" were the givers, and "They" were the takers.

This colonial mentality lasted until the end of the Second World War, with the bulk of the Canadian people showing little interest in the "Indian Question." The matter had a low political profile, clearly reflected in a trifling Indian administration of limited staff and budget. In any event, Indigenous Peoples were essentially thought to be the concern of the churches and of charitable organizations rather than a constitutional responsibility of the federal government. Apart from their spiritual role, the churches had also taken the lead in administering, on behalf of the federal government, Indigenous educational, health, and social welfare fields.

After the War, this perspective began to change. Government took on new roles in the economy and social welfare. An awakened sensibility emerged in thinking about "oppressed people," which included colonized people, Black people, and Indigenous Peoples. Colonialism and Imperialism were in retreat; racism came to be seen as an unacceptable attitude. The creation of the United Nations established an essential framework that reflected these new perspectives.

The first step was the United Nations' 1948 *Universal Declaration of Human Rights* with its pledge to recognize all humans as "born free and equal in dignity and rights regardless of nationality, place of residence, gender, national or ethnic origin, colour, religion, language, or any other status." This new framework legitimized struggles against all kinds of abuses of power, including the colonialism and racism affecting Indigenous people. In 2007, the UN went much further by vigorously rejecting racism and declaring a right to self-determination of Indigenous Peoples. Four countries, including Canada, voted against the declaration, only later to reverse themselves. Canada finally adopted this declaration in May 2016, as a first step in the Justin Trudeau government's program of national reconciliation with Indigenous Peoples.

Pierre Trudeau lived through this transformation, absorbing this movement toward universal human rights during his years of study in leading western universities. These liberal ideas had swept aside much of the teaching to which he had been exposed in Quebec. But he was not alone in responding to these winds of change.

Ironically, it was Conservative prime minister John Diefenbaker, who, as a strong defender of civil liberties, in his 1957 election campaign, defended Indigenous Peoples, criticized the Indian Affairs Branch and promised to remove some hated sections of the Indian Act. Many of these objectives were in conformity with Indigenous demands. He promised to establish an appeal mechanism to control the Indian Affairs Branch, to honour treaty obligations, and to grant Indigenous Peoples the right to vote. Granting this right to vote in 1960 was one of the most important reforms of the Diefenbaker government. The government also pressed the Indian Affairs Branch to speed up the process of helping Indigenous Peoples solve their own problems and to integrate them into Canadian society. These initiatives aroused broad public interest in Indigenous issues, heightened the search for effective policies, and prompted the creation of activist Indigenous associations. Hence, the ground was being laid for an ongoing Indigenous policy agenda to be subsequently passed on to Liberal governments under Lester Pearson in 1963 and Pierre Trudeau in 1968.

The Just Society for Aboriginal Peoples

It was Pierre Trudeau who then chose to pick up that agenda in earnest as his first major policy initiative only weeks after his election. He replaced Arthur Laing, the former minister in the Department of Indian Affairs and Northern Development (DIAND), with *two* ministers: Jean Chrétien, a thirty-four-year-old lawyer from Shawinigan Falls, and Robert K. Andras, a forty-seven-year-old businessman from Thunder Bay. On his appointment, Trudeau told Andras:

> This matter is very close to my heart. I feel we owe a great debt to the Indian people of Canada and I want you to play a major role in finding out, identifying that debt and recommending to the government the policies that will begin to meet our obligations, those obligations we may not have met in the past.[4]

Why did Trudeau appoint two ministers to deal with Indigenous policy? Given the high priority he had given the Indigenous question and his awareness of the huge demands this file would make on the Indian Affairs Branch, he installed both an institutional minister (Chrétien) and a roving, congenial, consultative minister (Andras) to manage the scores of meetings with Indigenous Peoples in the busy months ahead. Perhaps he was seeking too an equilibrium between the daring of youth and the wisdom of age? If so, he succeeded, but not in the expected way. The young and daring was not Chrétien but rather Andras, whose approach was decidedly radical, whereas Chrétien's kept close to the department and to his colleagues in the Liberal cabinet.

It didn't help matters when Andras declared, "As far as I'm concerned [the members of the department] are a bunch of Fascists. The deputy minister [J.A. Macdonald] wouldn't know an Indian if one walked down the street."[5] Unsurprisingly, relations between Chrétien and Andras soured. With the two ministers offering conflicting views of policy making, Indigenous Peoples strongly preferred Andras's "activism" to Chrétien's "traditionalism."

Of course, Trudeau had his own idea about what he thought should happen, which he pressed upon Chrétien, the newly minted minister. As Lawrence Martin explains, he asked: "Why not get out of the business of managing Indian Affairs altogether? Why not give the native peoples total freedom, like other minority groups in Canada?" Martin writes:

> The PM threw these ideas at Chrétien, and the minister — not being in much of a position to disagree — took the pronouncements to heart. It was a startling development. Two months into a portfolio he knew nothing about, the thirty-four-year-old minister was setting a course towards the most revolutionary change the department had ever seen. The plan, to be fleshed out over months of inquiry and consultation, was to abolish the Indian Act, dismantle the department of Indian Affairs,... end the reserve system, and give Indians equal status to everyone else.[6]

Trudeau followed through on the commitment of Arthur Laing, the former minister, to establish a series of meetings with Indigenous Peoples across

Canada. The first of eighteen of such meetings was held in Yellowknife on July 25, 1968. In his talk at this meeting, Chrétien set the tone by insisting that the government's purpose was to establish strong connections with the Indigenous Peoples and seek their advice and their critiques. The basic principle was that nothing would be "dictated from above." Yet "the cat was already among the pigeons. Trudeau knew what he wanted, and Chrétien knew it too."[7]

Indigenous Peoples: From "Citizens Minus" to "Citizens Plus"

While Trudeau was thinking on how to offer equality to Indigenous Peoples in a Just Society, others were busy making a case for Indigenous "special status." The architects of that vision emerged from an important research commission led by Harry B. Hawthorn, an Indigenous specialist and anthropologist at the University of British Columbia. Working from 1963 to 1967, the Hawthorn Group produced a two-volume report that came out in 1966 and 1967 entitled *A Survey of the Contemporary Indians of Canada: A Report on Economic, Political, Educational Needs and Policies*. This report was at the time the most comprehensive study ever carried out on the Indigenous Peoples of Canada.

The first volume is the most relevant here because it dealt with the political aspects of the question and the role of the Indian Affairs Branch, then went on to develop the social philosophy of a special status that came to be called "Citizens Plus." This notion can be attributed to Alan C. Cairns, professor of political science at the University of British Columbia, who was the major author of volume one.[8] Rejecting racist views that had prevailed for more than a century, the report declared: "[We] do not think that the Indian should be required to assimilate, neither in order to receive what he now needs nor at any future time."[9] On the contrary, "the general goal of the Report is to present the arguments establishing the right of Indians to be citizens plus and spell out some of the ways in which this status can be given practical momentum."[10]

The Hawthorn Group emphasized repeatedly the idea that "Indian people" were presently "citizens minus," by which they meant that they constituted Canada's most disadvantaged and marginalized population. The report showed that many lived in dire poverty, were often poorly educated, and lacked proper health care. The Hawthorn researchers attributed this situation to years of failed government policy, not least to the residential school system, which left students unprepared for participation in the contemporary economy. It was the fault of successive governments that the Indigenous Peoples became "citizens minus," or second-class citizens. And it ought to be the responsibility of future governments to correct this shameful situation by treating "Indians" as "Citizens Plus." They specified that one of the important causes of the present Indigenous situation was a systemic "dependency":

> [It] is a high degree of dependency that goes well beyond the dependency of the average person in today's complex welfare state because the sources of partial independence, primarily the ones linked to education and to income, are so much less for the Indians.[11]

Rejecting this legacy of dependency and the paternalism of the Indian Act and its administration, the report argued that for most Indians, supplemental external aid will be required. "Special facilities will be needed to ease the process of social adjustment.... Where possible these *should be provided by agencies other than the Indian Affairs Branch* [emphasis added]. However, if other agencies prove inadequate ... the Indian Affairs Branch must step in."[12]

The report said that a "national conscience" aiming at the establishment of social and economic equality between Indigenous and non-Indigenous people was needed. The Hawthorn Report did not recommend the elimination of the Indian Act or the Indian Affairs Branch, arguing instead for "reform rather than revolution." Conscious of the fact that the Indian Act had pluses and minuses, and that some Indigenous Peoples were for the Act and others against it, the Hawthorn Group argued that "the Indian Act, suitably modified where necessary, constitutes the most appropriate legislative vehicle for the development of Indian local government."[13]

There is no reason, claimed the report, to limit the political realm to the federal government when Canada has two levels of government. It seemed evident to them that all Canadian citizens should benefit fully from both levels of government. This, they argued, was even more unsatisfactory for the Indigenous Peoples, since welfare services fell under provincial legislation. Finally, the Hawthorn Group highlighted the absolute necessity of Indigenous Peoples' consent.

Carrying out all of this was important, yet action was difficult when the administration of Indian Affairs found itself with a seemingly endless rotation of seven ministers in different departments over the six years from the commission of the report in 1963 until the spring of 1969.[14] Morale was at a very low point, in part because many of the government's initiatives in that period turned out not to be successful.

In late October 1968, one of the most important meetings was a three-day symposium on issues facing Indigenous people, sponsored by Glendon College, at York University, in Toronto. It was a well-attended affair with speakers deeply involved in Indigenous issues. By far the most important was Harold Cardinal, a Cree born in High Prairie, Alberta, who at twenty-three years of age was already president of the Indian Association of Alberta and would remain in this post for an unprecedented nine terms. While in this position, he was instrumental in the formation of the National Indian Brotherhood and the forerunner of the Assembly of First Nations. Another important speaker with the regrettable name of John A. MacDonald was the new deputy minister of Indian affairs who had occupied his post a few months before the appointments of Chrétien and Andras. There was also a clerk of the Privy Council Office (PCO), Walter Rudnicki, who was well known for his support of Métis and Indigenous causes and very doubtful of the abilities of the bureaucrats in the DIAND. Rudnicki had no respect for experts, including the Hawthorn Group, whom he accused of being academics who visited many reserves but did not stay long enough to do a single in-depth study.[15] Understandably, Rudnicki was close to Andras, and both wholeheartedly supported the Indigenous cause.

At the Glendon forum, most participants were young students, and most of them were very supportive of Indigenous Peoples and clearly hostile toward the Department of Indian Affairs. In stark contrast but not surprisingly, MacDonald had to suffer almost continuous heckling from the audience. At one point, a student invited MacDonald to resign, and another student shredded a copy of the Indian Act as a sign of disgust at the department's handling of Indigenous issues. Similarly, Rudnicki severely criticized the efficacy of the policies used by the DIAND. Therefore, Rudnicki's talk was well received.

Harold Cardinal's address, however, was by far the most loudly applauded. Clearly in step with prevailing sentiments, Cardinal was already quickly emerging as a prominent Indigenous leader. After he had become president of the Indian Association of Alberta, Cardinal had proceeded to study at the University of Saskatchewan and later acquired a strong legal education, with a master's degree from Harvard University and a Doctorate of Law from UBC.

He strongly attacked the policies of the Department of Indian Affairs and argued for a thorough policy transformation, even suggesting a new division of tasks between Chrétien and Andras. Whereas Chrétien would take care of the administration of the department, a task force under Andras, which would include members of the National Indian Brotherhood, would oversee policy formation. Andras was quite in tune with Harold Cardinal's assertion that a precondition of success would be for the Canadian government "to commit itself morally, philosophically, and legislatively to honouring *fully* its agreements under Treaties signed with Indians, or where Treaties do not apply, to recognize and accept the *aboriginal* rights of these people [emphasis in original]."[16]

Clearly, there were numerous and contradictory perspectives on how to proceed effectively with Indigenous issues. Within Trudeau's cabinet, there were profound rifts between Chrétien and Andras. There were also rifts within the PCO: Rudnicki defended Cardinal's proposal of a task force including members of the National Indian Brotherhood, while Gordon Robertson, a senior advisor, opted for the creation of a Royal Commission. Chrétien rejected Robertson's view, since it would defer concrete action. The deputy minister, MacDonald, had another suggestion. He proposed something that would "capture Indian imagination and inspire their trust," some sort of "Marshall Plan for Indians."[17] His plan consisted in distributing one hundred million dollars to the various Indian bands and regional groups, who would hire experts to help them in developing their resources.

Harold Cardinal's Clever Strategic Invitation

But all these contradictory options were set aside when, at the end of October 1968, Harold Cardinal, acting in the name of the National Indian Brotherhood (NIB), invited Trudeau to host its forthcoming meeting in Ottawa in early December. In this way, the attention was swiftly taken away from the Ottawa mandarins and ministers and placed instead upon a high-stakes meeting with the prime minister and Indigenous leaders, who were themselves setting the agenda on their own terms.

Trudeau was already committed to attend a Human Rights Conference that was being held in Ottawa on the same date. Given how important human rights were to him, the choice between the two gatherings must have been difficult. Jim Davey and some other of Trudeau's advisors tried to dissuade Trudeau from accepting Cardinal's invitation to host the NIB luncheon meeting. They claimed, rightly, that the government didn't have a clear plan of action. This didn't dissuade Trudeau. The "Indian Question" was far too important to him.

The December conference seemed initially to be a success. Indigenous leaders were able to set out their position emphasizing treaty rights to a broad public audience, while Trudeau and his cabinet adopted a respectful listening posture. The press coverage of the luncheon was positive. It was widely reported that most delegates from the various provincial and regional Indigenous organizations were pleased with the talks and especially with their discussions with the prime minister. The general feeling that came out of the luncheon was that this was a government that would listen carefully to Indigenous opinions before making decisions. Trudeau asked his two ministers to take account of opinions expressed by Indigenous leaders.

Yet beneath the surface, there was considerable skepticism too amongst some Indigenous leaders, particularly from Chief George Manuel, later to be president of the NIB from 1970 to 1976 and founding leader of the World Council of Indigenous Peoples in 1975. His view of the meeting was dark, not to say insulting. He believed that nothing positive had been done and that Indigenous Peoples should not expect anything positive from this government or from any future one. In a brief statement, he attacked Trudeau and expressed what he felt could be expected from Canadian governments:

> Most of the Indian Chiefs at the feast knew from the Prime Minister's statement that some sinister plans were taking place within Government.... I believe what took place at the meeting was a "replay" of what happened ... with our forefathers in earlier history ... to persuade them to sign away our Indian territory.[18]

Chief Manuel's views were not shared by most of the Chiefs, who instead expressed their pleasure at having attended the conference. Nonetheless, Manuel's and Harold Cardinal's skepticism would soon come to prevail among Indigenous leaders and become the dominant force in the later fight against the 1969 White Paper. They were joined by David Courchene, the leader of the Manitoba Indian Brotherhood, who demanded recognition of Indigenous Rights and treaty rights. From this moment on, it rapidly became clear that, for Indigenous Peoples, a meaningful dialogue with the government would only make sense when their special rights would be recognized and honoured.

Trudeau, who was a firm believer of the principle of the rule of law, reacted in a restrained manner to the nature of these claimed rights. At this stage, he shared the doubts of the lawyer of the task force created by the NIB, who highlighted the absence of legislative and executive declarations and the lack of legal precedent for the notion of Indigenous Rights. What did this notion really mean? Did it mean that Indigenous Peoples would take their ancestral lands back? On the other hand, legally enforceable claims, that is, treaty rights, should certainly be honoured. In a speech made in Vancouver on August 8, 1969, Trudeau clearly expressed his view on these rights:

> We will recognize ... forms of contract which have been made with the Indian people by the Crown. And we will try to bring justice in that area. And this will mean that perhaps the treaties shouldn't go on forever. It is inconceivable I think that in a given society, one section of the society have a treaty with the other sections of the society. We must all be equal under the laws and we must not

> sign treaties amongst ourselves and many of these treaties indeed would have less and less significance in the future anyhow.[19]

These thoughts on Indigenous rights were far from reflecting the understanding of Indigenous Peoples. But by June 1969, the federal policy was ready to be presented to the House of Commons. The day before the policy was to be announced, Indigenous leaders met with Jean Chrétien in Ottawa for an informal session. They were invited to sit in the gallery of the House of Commons on June 25, 1969, to hear the *Statement of the Government of Canada on Indian Policy* (known as the "1969 White Paper"). Jean Chrétien, minister of Indian affairs and northern development, stood in the House to say:

> Mr. Speaker, I am pleased to place the government's statement on Indian policy before the house. The statement outlines the views the government brings to the consultations which must now be carried on with the Indian people and the provincial governments.[20]

Chrétien emphasized that the policy was a proposal and not a binding statement. It was, rather, a response to Indigenous demands and a crucial step toward meaningful consultations. In the next few months, Chrétien, Trudeau, and other members of the government travelled across the country to present the new policy to Canadians, especially Indigenous Peoples.

At first, the response to the 1969 White Paper by the press, by politicians, and by the Canadian public at large was positive. The policy was described in laudatory terms, such as "well written," "eloquent," "a major breakthrough," but also as "revolutionary" and "radical." The general commentary focused on Trudeau as the mastermind behind the policy. Reportedly, Trudeau had spent more time on this policy than on any other issue during his first year of office. One day after the policy announcement, on June 26, 1969, Anthony Westell of the *Vancouver Sun* saluted enthusiastically the arrival of the government's statement:

> Prime Minister Pierre Elliott Trudeau celebrated the anniversary of his election triumph Wednesday by placing before the Commons the first of the radical measures he has promised to achieve a Just Society — the new Indian policy.
>
> The statement says bluntly that for more than a 100 years Canada has pursued policies of discrimination — or apartness, or apartheid — toward its Indian peoples.
>
> This is a searing indictment of a century of Canadian government paternalism, of 100 years of the Indian Act. Any cabinet which arrived at such a diagnosis of the Indian condition obviously had to abandon the old policies and to strive for new solutions.

In Vancouver, a few weeks later, on August 8, 1969, Trudeau highlighted the Canadian government's long-standing mishandling of the Indigenous Peoples and explained his government's proposal. The *Statement of the Government of Canada on Indian Policy* would not be imposed on anyone, but it declared without ambiguity its point of view:

> The Government believes that its policies must lead to the full, free and non-discriminatory participation of the Indian people in Canadian society. Such a goal requires a break with the past. It requires that the Indian people's role of dependence be replaced by a role of equal status, opportunity and responsibility, a role they can share with all other Canadians.[21]

Despite the assurances that the policy would not be imposed, critiques afterward treated the policy as an imposition. Yet the *Statement* was not a definitive declaration of the intentions of the government but, rather, an offer of the government to the Indigenous Peoples. It was intended as a launching-pad toward a better understanding of relations between Indigenous people and non-Indigenous people, and between various Indigenous groups and the Canadian governments.

Trudeau's *Statement* has often been criticized as a form of shock treatment meant to assimilate Indigenous Peoples as quickly as possible. These critics believe that Trudeau's basic premise was the historical one: that a "backward" people could benefit from their close encounter with a more "progressive" majority society. In other words, Trudeau was committing the same form of racism as so many other government leaders in the past century and a half. Yet the spirit of these introductory words, which permeates the entire *Statement*, is relentlessly inclusive and egalitarian.

From his early Christian education, Trudeau acquired a profound belief that all humans were equal in the eyes of God, and later in his adult years, he saw this as a humanistic principle: all humans deserve an equal degree of respect regardless of their race, religion, ethnicity, gender, and sexual preference. This didn't mean that Trudeau believed that all humans were alike. Nor did it mean, as is frequently asserted even in serious studies on Trudeau, that he was an inveterate "individualist" who forgot that humans were social beings who tend to act collectively within organized groups. It meant, rather, that differences between humans should be accepted and even celebrated as one of the essential foundations of a Just Society. This explains, for example, his attachment to the notion of multiculturalism and his goal of fostering a multicultural Canada.

In a democratic and liberal society, respect for the law was, to him, the political translation of the moral equality of humans. As a result, he rejected the very notion of various categories of citizens being treated differently under the law. The *Statement* asserts this idea as follows:

> The government believes that all men and women have equal rights. It is determined that all shall be treated fairly and that no one shall be shut out of Canadian life, and especially that no one shall be shut out because of his race. This belief is the basis for the Government's determination to open the doors of opportunity to all Canadians, to remove the barriers which impede the development of people, of regions and of the country.

> The goals of the Indian people cannot be set by others; they must spring from the Indian community itself — but the government can create a framework within which all persons and groups can seek their own goals.[22]

After having repeatedly expressed the fact that nothing would be done without the full agreement of Indigenous Peoples, the *Statement* presented the main elements of the framework being offered:

- Repeal the Indian Act and take such legislative steps as may be necessary to enable Indigenous control of "lands reserved for Indians" and to acquire title to them.
- Propose to the governments of the provinces that they take the same responsibility for the Indigenous Peoples as they have taken for other citizens in their jurisdictions.
- Make substantial funds available for Indigenous economic development as an interim measure.
- Wind up part of the DIAND which deals with Indian Affairs.
- Appoint a Commissioner to consult with the Indigenous Peoples and to study and recommend acceptable procedures for the adjudication of claims.[23]

Surprisingly, the harshest critiques presented by Indigenous Peoples zeroed in on the notion that, in its entirety, the *Statement* was focused on less pressing issues, such as the immediate repeal of the Indian Act, and ignored Canada's failure to respect treaty rights. Given the longstanding demand for overturning the Indian Act, this seemed hard to understand. But at the time, it was a question of priorities for Indigenous Peoples: whether to pursue land claims and self-government agreements on the basis of existing Indigenous treaty rights or throw off the hated Indian Act. The latter was a tempting, but possibly premature, option. After all, the Hawthorn Report had argued for the retention of a reformed Indian Affairs department to assist Indigenous Peoples in any practical road to reform.

Yet Indigenous Peoples had long demanded the repeal of the Act. In a national bestseller published in 2018 entitled *21 Things You May Not Know About the Indian Act*, Bob Joseph provided a thorough history of the fraught interactions of the Indigenous Peoples and the Indian Act from the day of its inception. He accepted the widespread criticism of the Act and thought it did more harm than good. He showed that the very structure of the Act was ill-conceived, quoting Laurence Paul, chair of the Atlantic Policy Congress of First Nations Chiefs Secretariat, who wrote in 2009, "The *Indian Act* has attempted to displace our inherent authority as leaders and has eroded our traditions, culture, and belief systems. It does not reflect our needs and aspirations. It has also not kept pace with principles of modern and accountable governments."[24]

The Act treated "Indians" like children who were unable to behave properly without the guidance of a paternalistic government. It discriminated against Indigenous women and their children by stripping them of "Indian status" if they married non-Indigenous men. Yet another hated paternalistic feature was the Act's interdiction of the Potlatch, a ceremony integral to the culture and spiritual traditions of various Indigenous Peoples living on the Northwest coast and in parts of the interior of the western subarctic. Similarly objectionable was government control of the access to liquor. Indigenous Peoples were not allowed to attend functions where liquor was served or to frequent pool halls, being directed instead to other, approved, amusements and activities.

Worse still was the pass system that the Canadian government had put into place a year after the Riel Rebellion 1885 to reassure settlers and immigrants to the Canadian West.[25] This story is described in the recent book *Valley of the Birdtail*, by Andrew Stobo Sniderman and Douglas Sanderson, showing how "Indians" required official permission from Indian agents before leaving a reserve. The authors set out the bitter outcome:

> Anyone caught off the reserve without a pass was liable to be arrested for vagrancy or trespass and forcibly returned. The system transformed every unauthorized traveller into a fugitive and every reserve into a holding pen.... [26]

> In the decades to come, the cumulative effects of the pass system on Indigenous communities were devastating. It was a barrier to finding work, customers, or other opportunities off reserve. It also choked traditional education and culture by limiting opportunities to gather for ceremonies. By design, reserves became an archipelago of open-air prisons.[27]

The most loathsome part of the Indian Act was the establishment of residential schools. Indigenous children were frequently taken from their family and culture and then repeatedly told that their spirituality and beliefs were pagan and primitive. In these schools, the mandate of the administrators was to ensure that the children would learn to read, write, understand, and speak English. If they spoke their own language, they were severely punished. The fundamental goal of the schools was embodied in the popularly used phrase, "kill the Indian in the child." Far too often, children did *die* in these schools, with their bodies registered, but then buried, often in unmarked graves.

With this history of the Indian Act, might it therefore be possible to look at the government's 1969 White Paper as a step, however small, in the right direction? Why did the Indigenous Peoples then so massively come to reject the government's project? As we have noted earlier, their response to the White Paper was initially mixed.[28] At first, as one would expect, there were positive and negative views. But very rapidly, their voices became unified — all against the White Paper. First, let us look at some of the rare positive voices.

Len Marchand was the first Indigenous member of the Liberal Party. As such, he became an important spokesperson for the government's view of the White Paper. His basic position was in tune with Trudeau's. Another strong Indigenous supporter of the White Paper was William I.C. Wuttunee, the head of the National Indian Council (NIC). He passionately believed that Canadian citizenship and the abolition of "Indian" reserves would solve his peoples' problems. He tried to spread his views amongst the people of his home province of Saskatchewan and wrote a well-researched and controversial book entitled *Ruffled Feathers: Indians in Canadian Society.* Wuttunee claimed that Harold Cardinal, Chief of the Indian Association of Alberta, leader of the "Red Power" movement, and author of *The Unjust Society*, made a mistake when he refused to negotiate with the federal government until the treaties were recognized. In so doing, Cardinal had led Indigenous Peoples on a reactionary and dangerous path to attempt to remake history. To Wuttunee, it was "not possible to turn back the hands of history or to rewrite those hundred-year-old documents."[29]

Wuttunee bemoaned the fact that "Indians are now big business, and everyone is scrambling to get to the top of these organizations so that they can help spend the funds."[30] Cardinal and his Indian Association of Alberta were champions in this new race to get money. For example, in 1972, the Association obtained four million dollars from the federal government. More importantly, Cardinal paid himself a huge salary plus expenses of about fifty thousand dollars, and many other leaders received similar impressive sums. Wuttunee considered it unjust that this association and its leaders "should pay themselves such exorbitant salaries, bearing in mind the poverty in which so many Indian people live." He also accused Cardinal and his "Red Power" group of having fostered the rise of nepotism and favouritism in the organizations and in local band councils. He complained of being personally "banned from the area when I spoke in favour of the government's White Paper on Indian Policy, without having given me the opportunity of presenting my arguments."[31]

Walter Dieter, the first president of the NIB, found both good and bad points in the policy. Even Harold Cardinal found something positive and welcomed the idea of overturning the entrenched paternalism in the Department of Indian Affairs. But the degree of antagonism against the White Paper rose very rapidly. The very next day after it was announced, Dave Courchene, a leader of the Manitoba Indian Brotherhood, denounced the policy and accused the government of having failed to properly consult the Indigenous leaders:

> Once again, the future of the Indian people has been dealt with in a high-handed and arbitrary manner. We have not been consulted, we have been advised of decisions already taken.[32]

The notion that the government misled the Indigenous Peoples and didn't consult them became the main reasons to reject the White Paper. Both Chrétien and Trudeau tried in vain to argue the government's good faith. As opposition increased, Chrétien tried to demonstrate that the White Paper was a proposal for further discussion and negotiation. Far from wanting to force anything on the Indigenous Peoples, the government was committed to discussions. In an article published in the *Globe and Mail* of July 8, 1969, Chrétien wrote:

> We will not push anything down anyone's throat. We will not abandon anyone or any problem. We will be flexible. We do want to discuss.
>
> *The Government believes the proposals are the right ones* [emphasis added]. It is committed to discussion, negotiating, consulting, to make them the right ones. It wants the chance to do this and it seeks the full and continuing involvement and understanding of those whose decisions will affect its chances.[33]

Unfortunately, just a few of the words in this article had a huge impact on the Indigenous opposition. In the eyes of some leaders, the notion that the government "believed the proposals were the right ones" meant that the government was not "committed to discussion." This increased their strong beliefs that the government, always trying to appease Indigenous opponents, was duping them.

Three days later, on July 11, 1969, the first debate was held on the White Paper in the House of Commons. Members of Parliament sought confirmation that the policy was a proposal and would not be implemented in the face of Indigenous opposition. Chrétien argued that the failure of the existing system had demanded considerable changes in the relations between the government and Indigenous Peoples. Chrétien reiterated the view that the policy was simply a proposal and that the government was committed to discussion and consultation and had no intention whatever to rush the implementation of it. But Indigenous leaders were not convinced of Chrétien's assurances nor of Trudeau's.

In an important speech given in Vancouver on August 8, 1969, Trudeau radicalized the Indigenous opposition instead of appeasing it. He claimed that after having studied thoroughly the "Indian question," the government had come up with two choices: the first choice was to retain the conventional way of dealing with Indigenous issues — which would barely, if at all, ameliorate the present situation — and the second choice was to replace the old system with one giving Indigenous Peoples full status in society. Once again, Trudeau defended the idea that treating all Canadians as fairly as possible did not mean the elimination of special needs nor the imposition of certain cultural values. However, it could be that the words he chose in his speech were ambiguous. He felt that the demand of "special rights," which Indigenous leaders requested, were incongruous in a democratic and just society. Not only did he feel that *all* Canadian citizens should have equal rights under the law, but he also claimed that his government couldn't recognize Indigenous Rights because no society can be built on "might-have-beens."

In a reply to a letter by Dave Courchene, Trudeau tried to erase the ambiguity in his speech. He denied he was disavowing the treaties and reminded Courchene that he had personally supported the policy. With respect to the demand of Indigenous Rights, he accepted that the government should honour "treaty rights."[34] Furthermore, he wrote that "if the Indian character can survive only by protection of special legislation, then it will disappear of its own account.... But our diversity must continue on its own merits, not artificially, through special legislation or by seeking the protection of history."[35]

Trudeau's perspective angered Indigenous leaders and especially the leaders of the NIB even further. Just as Chrétien's failed attempts to convince them that the government was open to discussion fell on deaf ears, so too did Trudeau's. He was not believed. His conception of "rights" was not only rejected but became the focal point of the battle against the White Paper. As Sally Weaver writes: "Indian leaders felt duped by the consultation process [and] The White Paper became the single most powerful catalyst of the Indian nationalist movement, launching it into a determined force for nativism."[36]

Harold Cardinal's Counterattack on the White Paper

From the final national consultation meeting held in Ottawa on April 28, 1969, to the release of the White Paper, Harold Cardinal and George Manuel worked behind the scenes to encourage Indigenous Peoples to reject the government's agenda. Their first success was to push Walter Dieter out of the position of chair of the consultation meeting of the NIB and to convince the delegates to replace him with Manuel. This was easy to do. They further plotted to kick Dieter out of the NIB at the forthcoming July meeting in Vancouver.[37] As we have seen, Walter Dieter did not reject the White Paper; indeed, he openly declared that there was both good and bad in it. But this was insufficient for Cardinal and Manuel, who were radically against the White Paper's focus on the Indian Act. Cardinal claimed that his position was backed by the clear mandate of the Alberta delegation and from the Alberta people: the Alberta people had given a clear instruction to the Alberta delegation that "the Indian Act was not the issue and that they should talk only of their rights — rights that had been denied to them for over a hundred years."[38]

There is no factual evidence, however, that the "Alberta people" had given any mandate to the NIB. In fact, we don't know if the delegates even voted on this proposition and whether there were any objections. What we do know is that just after the release of the White Paper, a flow of letters and telegrams were sent to MPs by Indigenous leaders, associations, and bands. This flow transformed radically the attitude of the Indigenous Peoples as well as the media toward the White Paper. We also know that the delegates did go a step further and proposed the creation of an organization that would be called the National Committee on Indian Rights and Treaties. Once that proposal was accepted, the leaders of the NIB presented to Chrétien a bill for over half a million dollars to fund this new organization. Shocked by this huge demand, Chrétien merely agreed to study the matter.

Such were the backroom politics, but the intellectual rebuttal of the White Paper would fall to the young, gifted Harold Cardinal. In two publications in 1969, one satirically entitled *The Unjust Society* and another colloquially known as the "Red Paper," Cardinal dismissed the White Paper as bad policy hidden behind meaningless sweet words. On the first page of his *Unjust Society*, Harold Cardinal described the White Paper as a "thinly disguised programme of extermination through assimilation."[39] Such was the nature of his intellectual demolition designed to convince Indigenous representatives to reject Trudeau's White Paper.

Cardinal was, as we've noted, a highly educated and cultured person, as well as an excellent writer and speaker. Just as importantly, he was a born leader. He put these gifts to good use in his roles as an Albertan Indigenous leader and as a founder of the NIB, the forerunner of the Assembly of First Nations. In 1982, at the time of the patriation of the Canadian Constitution, he was the vice-chief of the Assembly of First Nations. In the late 1960s, his words had galvanized Indigenous Peoples into action. The result was a complete about-face by the federal government on the policies of the White Paper in the early 1970s.

Cardinal's added gift for satire was displayed in the titles of these books, turning Trudeau's promise of a "Just Society" into an "Unjust Society" and a "White Paper" into a "Red Paper." *The Unjust Society*, written to tell the story of Indigenous Peoples from an Indigenous perspective, appeared late in 1969. The second shorter publication, unofficially called the Red Paper, was published in June 1970 and was also approved by the NIB. It was a point-by-point critique of the White Paper accompanied by a point-by-point rejoinder. Its official title was *Citizens Plus*, as a salute to the Hawthorn Report.

In 1999, Cardinal decided to publish a new edition of *The Unjust Society* with an introduction meant to assess the situation of Indigenous Peoples thirty years after the 1969 White Paper. He wondered if the tough struggles against the White Paper had been worth the results obtained. He wrote that "unfortunately, at the core, the issues this book identified in the late 1960s are issues still unresolved today."[40] Cardinal's reassessment of his participation helps us to understand the Indigenous struggles with a thirty-year time lapse.

In his books of 1969 and 1970, Cardinal sought two objectives: 1) to define the "real" demands of the Indigenous Peoples, rather than those presented by the government, and 2) to convince his people of the necessity of struggling against the White Paper. An important demand was the rejection of the paternalism of the DIAND. He claimed that they constituted "a dictatorial bureaucracy [which] has eroded our rights, atrophied our culture and robbed us of simple human dignity."[41] On this issue he further wrote:

> These faceless people in Ottawa, a comparatively small group, perpetually unknown, have sat at their desks eight hours a day, five days a week, for over a century, and decided just about everything that will ever happen to a Canadian Indian. They have laid down the policy, the rules, and the regulations on all matters affecting native peoples.[42]

Cardinal's critique of the White Paper put the Trudeau government's policy in the same bag as all preceding governments. And throughout the book, Cardinal always presented the Indigenous as honourable people with high principles and the white man invariably as "a fork-tongued cheat." This Manichean portrait is simplistic, just as is a uniform history with no distinctions. Yet it most certainly constitutes a powerful political discourse.

By autumn 1969, the government had failed to convince Indigenous Peoples and their leaders of its intention to discuss the policy. This led the Indigenous organizations to decide to take their time to examine the policy in detail and to prepare counterproposals. They demanded that, until they were ready with their own proposals, no steps to implement the White Paper be taken.

Early in June 1970, one year after the release of the White Paper, the counterproposal prepared by Harold Cardinal was ready and approved by the Indian Association of Alberta. On June 3, Indigenous leaders gathered in Ottawa to debate the adoption of the counterproposal by the NIB. After making a few minor corrections, they endorsed the Alberta paper, officially entitled *Citizens Plus* and also called the Red Paper. Trudeau had just returned from Australia, where he had spent some time studying the situation of Indigenous Peoples there. His first reaction with respect to the Canadian situation was that if the Indigenous and the non-Indigenous didn't want the proposed policy, "We're not going to force it down their throats."

A Ceremonial Setting Worthy of History

Cardinal had prepared a striking and original strategy for the presentation of the counterproposal. He had several objectives in mind. First, he wanted to present the Indigenous proposal in front of Trudeau and his cabinet; second, he wanted to be accompanied by several Indigenous Chiefs and Elders; and third, he wanted the presentation to take place in the Parliament Building. All these demands were not easy to achieve, especially since Cardinal didn't even make an appointment with Trudeau. But these handicaps were overcome quickly by obtaining some inside help from pro-Indigenous activists, such as Robert Andras from the PMO and Walter Rudnicki from the PCO. The meeting with Trudeau and his cabinet took place very promptly on June 4, 1970, in the beautiful and historic Railway Committee Room of Parliament.

After the introduction of the members of Trudeau's cabinet and the Indigenous delegates, the NIB launched into its carefully rehearsed presentation of the Red Paper. After a brief prayer by an Elder, two Chiefs in traditional regalia walked up to the cabinet table. One handed a copy of the White Paper to Chrétien as a sign of rejection of the government's policy, and the other handed the Red Paper to Trudeau as a sign of their final chosen policy direction. This solemn, unspoken ceremonial gesture captured the profound meaning of this historical moment.

Harold Cardinal's later description of the proceedings stressed two notions. First, that the relationship between the government and Indigenous Peoples depended on the recognition of Indigenous Rights. On this point, he suggested that to break the impasse on Indigenous and Treaty Rights, a truly impartial Claims Commissioner should be appointed after consultation with Indigenous Peoples. Second, that the government's consultation and negotiating team had to be replaced by a new consultative system acceptable to both the NIB and the government. What mattered most, said Cardinal, is that the government should no longer be inflexible.

As the meeting proceeded, everything was going well. The discussions were respectful on both sides, and Cardinal was applauded repeatedly both by the delegates and observers — especially when he spoke of the historic importance of the meeting itself. This feeling of being at an important moment in history was shared by those present. The Indigenous leaders and the government had finally found a way to discuss and negotiate peaceably and effectively. Then Trudeau spoke, and all the people in the room could not believe their ears. His statement was close to an apology, and he was cheered when he admitted that after all the work on the White Paper, "the Indian people have looked at this and they have said, it's no good."[43]

Trudeau went on to explain what happened and shared the blame with Jean Chrétien and the many other dedicated people who had worked with diligence and integrity with the government:

> I'm sure that we were very naïve in some of the statements we made in the paper. We had perhaps the prejudices of small "l" liberals and white men who thought that equality meant the same law for everybody.... But we have learnt in the process that perhaps we were a bit too theoretical, we were a bit too abstract, we were not, as Mr. Cardinal suggests, perhaps pragmatic enough or understanding enough, and that's fine. We are here to discuss this.[44]

Two specific remarks in this statement help us understand why Trudeau abandoned the White Paper. In recognizing that small "l" liberals can be very naive and have prejudices, he acknowledged that everyone can make mistakes. And in his last sentence accepting Mr. Cardinal's critique, Trudeau showed that the foundation of liberalism is the recognition and acceptance of the other. This "other" could be an individual or a group of persons. And Trudeau, who strongly believed in the rule of law, accepted the views of Cardinal when the matter at issue was precisely the law. In other words, Trudeau had just been reminded by Cardinal that Indigenous Peoples, not unlike other groups of people, could very well have a system of law or a culture that was different from those of non-Indigenous Canadians. Trudeau was reminded by Cardinal that a true "liberal" would accept the "other." Having learned an important lesson from Cardinal, he tipped his hat to him in his last few words: "I hear you, from now on let us talk to each other ... let us listen to each other and get the best we can to satisfy the needs of the Indian peoples."

Trudeau would prove true to his word. Despite his skepticism over special collective rights, Trudeau proved in future years a willing partner in constitutionalizing Indigenous Rights. He was the first prime minister to take on the "Indian Question" comprehensively as a matter of social justice and the first to recognize existing Indigenous and Treaty Rights (Rights of the Aboriginal Peoples of Canada) in section 35 of the Constitution in 1982. It was doubtless a curious irony that his Liberal White Paper would boomerang, advancing instead the cause of collective Indigenous Rights in Canada.

So "The Unfinished Tapestry" — Chrétien's apt metaphor — would continue. Soon things took the direction that Indigenous leaders had demanded: that priority be given to Indigenous Rights and treaty rights. The 1973 Supreme Court ruling in the *Calder v. the Queen* case led to the recognition of Indigenous title as a legal right. About a decade later came recognition of the "Rights of the Aboriginal Peoples of Canada" in the Constitution Act, 1982. A further decade saw Indigenous participation in constitutional negotiations alongside government leaders and provision for Indigenous constitutional self governance in the 1992 Charlottetown Accord — a large unwieldy package of proposed changes, subsequently voted down in a national referendum. It's a long story that runs like a thread through Trudeau's life. A transformative wave of change for Indigenous Peoples had come to Canada in large part as a direct consequence of the sincere attention given to this matter by Pierre Elliott Trudeau.

And so, it went — a wave of change that has not, of course, resolved centuries of racial injustice. The Royal Commission on Aboriginal Peoples, Gordon Robertson's proposal to the 1968 Trudeau Cabinet, came to fruition in the 1990s, the most comprehensive study of Indigenous Peoples ever undertaken. Its recommendations pointed the way to better understanding and suggested steps to further reform. The *Calder* case prompted the Trudeau government to launch long and complicated negotiations with the British Columbia Nisga'a Tribal Council that led, in 1999–2000, to the Nisga'a achieving control of about two thousand square kilometres of its former territory. And in the same year, 1999, came the largest devolution of territory to Indigenous Peoples in history: the new territory of Nunavut carved out of the former Northwest Territories.

Steps toward national reconciliation continue, often painfully, as in the unfolding of the shocking story of Indigenous children's deaths in residential schools. Confronting the institutional actors in this tragedy goes on, with even Pope Francis being called to account. History, unable to unmake the injustices of the past, so often moves glacially, but at least it appears to be moving in a better direction.

FIVE

The Scourge of Political Violence in Quebec

> "Well, there's a lot of bleeding hearts around who just don't like to see people with helmets and guns. All I can say is, go on and bleed, but it's more important to keep law and order in this society than to be worried about weak-kneed people."
>
> "How far would you go?" a journalist asked.
>
> Trudeau replied: "Just watch me."[1]

THIS MEMORABLE EXCHANGE, ON OCTOBER 13, 1970, CAPTURED PRIME MINISTER Pierre Trudeau's famous response to the politics of terrorism. "Just watch me" was said calmly and simply not, as widely imagined, in an arrogant or flippant manner. The remark arose after a conversation Trudeau had with CBC reporter Tim Ralfe, who had questioned armed soldiers in the streets. Trudeau asked Ralfe what he thought should be done in the face of political violence in Quebec. This question went unanswered. Yet governments hadn't the luxury of silence or inaction. They were confronting rising FLQ violence that had engulfed Quebec for almost a decade.

In contrast, Trudeau's response suggested resolute defiance and hinted at a yet unannounced, well-calculated plan of action. It was clear the Canadian state would not submit to criminal intimidation, nor would it "lose its head" in a crisis. Moreover, he was saying most emphatically that a liberal democratic state will surely not hesitate to use armed force to protect law and order when confronting groups brazenly using violence to promote their political ends. In short, there would be no "weak-kneed" yielding to the criminal approach to politics. From the outset then, Pierre Trudeau was deadly serious in carefully managing and seeing through Canada's most serious confrontation with terrorism.

In the 1960s and 1970s, revolutionary movements employing terrorism and violence appeared throughout the world. Quebec was no exception. Whether we consider the Basque ETA terrorist group in Spain, the armed Corsican movement for independence from France, the sectarian IRA in Northern Ireland promoting union with Ireland, or the armed wing of the ANC fighting apartheid in South Africa, it was not unusual that terrorism would be used as a tool of politics. In the case of Quebec, a left-wing politics of violence against capitalism had become entwined in the struggle for Quebec independence that mushroomed into prominence during the Quiet Revolution. The October Crisis of 1970 represented the climax of this revolutionary movement and its swift, subsequent denouement. After the crisis passed, the politics of separatism would go on to dominate Quebec politics over the next quarter century, but it would do so in peaceful political debate, free of bombs, kidnappings, and intimidation. That would be Quebecers' good fortune, after enduring the dark days of the October Crisis, and they would thereafter always choose the politics of non-violence, even when deciding the "national question."

The FLQ and the October Crisis

With the arrival of the Quiet Revolution, the 1960s saw a decade of vigorous electoral politics. But there were always those who strongly believed from the start that the only way to solve Quebec's problems was through a combination of violence and revolution. The most important promotor of this option was the FLQ, which was launched on March 8, 1963, by a group of people ready and willing to "save" Quebec through terrorist activities. Their members were inspired by decolonization writers like Frantz Fanon, who had argued that "decolonization is always a violent phenomenon."[2] The historian D'Arcy Jenish showed that the FLQ had come to see Quebec as "not a province but a colony, and French-speaking Quebeckers as not a minority [in Canada] but a colonized people, and the English not as fellow citizens but occupiers."[3] This was the mindset that guaranteed a politics of violence in Quebec and laid the seeds of the so-called October Crisis.

That climax came with the kidnapping of James Cross, a British diplomat serving as Trade Commissioner to promote commerce between Canada and Great Britain. The FLQ assailants, fully armed, had worked out a plot that left Cross and his household surprised and helpless, while they shielded themselves with a secure exit plan. Early on the morning of October 5, 1970, one of them rang the doorbell while Mr. Cross and his wife were upstairs chatting and getting dressed. Assuming it was probably Quebec Hydro come to read the meter, the Portuguese maid, Amelia Santos, answered the door while cradling her baby in one arm. A so-called delivery man stood there, holding a long and beautifully wrapped package as he announced, "Birthday present for Mr. Cross," and asked for a signature.

When the maid answered that she didn't have a pen, the terrorist said that he had one, then pulled a revolver from his pocket and entered the house. Two accomplices who were hiding outside the house came in. One of them tore the paper off the package, pulled out a submachine gun and stood guard at the door. The others mounted the stairs, ordered Cross to lie face down on the floor and then dressed and handcuffed him. He was then carried outside and pushed into a taxi between the front and back seats. Five to ten minutes later, he was moved into another car and taken to the second floor of a house, where he was put on a mattress — that is where he spent the next fifty-nine days. The kidnappers then issued communiqués with threats to kill Cross if their demands weren't met within forty-eight hours.[4]

What were these demands? Insisting on a halt to police searches and the delivery of gold worth half a million dollars, their principal ransom demand was the public broadcasting of the FLQ Manifesto and the release of twenty-three "political prisoners" (convicted FLQ criminals) and their safe passage to Cuba or Algeria. According to recent declassified documents, "Canadian intelligence had long suspected ties between Cuba and the FLQ with a 1964 study reporting that the Cuban consul in Montreal had suggested that Quebec 'should be made a socialist state by revolutionary means' at a separatist meeting."[5] It was well known that FLQ co-founder George Schoeters had met Fidel Castro as early as 1959 and had travelled to Cuba several times afterward, prompting suspicions that the country was becoming a base for FLQ training. In any event, just three days after Cross was taken, intense negotiations began in Havana between Canadian chargé d'affaires Bill Warden and Cuban foreign minister Raúl Roa Garcia. The following day, after Mr. Roa had consulted with Fidel Castro, the Cuban government agreed to co-operate. The foreign minister said that Quebec independence would be "very unfortunate," as it would reduce Quebec to an "island," and leave Canada less able to stand up to the United States. Mr. Roa added that Cuba appreciated Canada's "independent policy towards Cuba," as Canada had not joined the American sanctions on the country.[6]

Cuba offered "carte blanche" co-operation to Canada. Indeed, it offered the country's consulate in Montreal for the transfer of FLQ terrorists to Cuba and the release of the kidnapped. The Canadian pavilion at Expo was made an extension of the Cuban consulate for this purpose. So was laid the basic plan for a transfer arrangement that indeed did take place on December 3, 1970, after Mr. Cross and his kidnappers were found. Cross and his captors were whisked in a police convoy to Expo and thence to the airport. On the plane, one of the kidnappers, Jacques Cossette-Trudel, told diplomat Ormond Dier that they never considered killing Mr. Cross and that his radicalism stemmed from seeing "social and economic deprivation" in east-end Montreal and from reading the radical writings of Frantz Fanon.[7]

On October 10, 1970, five days after James Cross's kidnapping, it was Pierre Laporte's turn to be seized. Laporte had been a journalist with *Le Devoir* from 1945 to 1961. During those years, he published numerous articles criticizing the Duplessis government. When Jean Lesage announced in 1969 that he would step down as leader of Quebec's Liberal Party, Laporte ran to succeed him, but he lost the leadership election to Robert Bourassa, a fellow member of cabinet. Premier Bourassa recognized Pierre Laporte's talent and recommended that he be appointed parliamentary leader, with responsibility for the senior ministries of labour and immigration. In short, Laporte was about as high-profile a politician as could be imagined, short of the premier of Quebec himself.

On that October day in 1970, four terrorists — Paul and Jacques Rose, Francis Simard, and Bernard Lortie — approached Laporte while he was playing football with his nephew in a field opposite his front lawn and forced him into their vehicle at gunpoint. They held him hostage, demanding the release of twenty-three "political prisoners" in exchange for his freedom. This catapulted the situation into a full-scale emergency that generated widespread public fear. Unable to track down the terrorists and stretched to the limit trying to protect public property, both the mayor of Montreal, Jean Drapeau, and the premier of Quebec, Robert Bourassa, requested the assistance of the Canadian Army and special emergency powers. Ottawa sent in military assistance but delayed the request for emergency powers, hoping that existing laws would prove adequate. After persistent pressure from Quebec authorities, amid growing public concern, the federal government finally agreed to these requests. Using the only available emergency law available at the time, it declared "a state of apprehended insurrection" under the War Measures Act (WMA) on October 16.

This was the first time that such legislation had ever been used outside of actual war time. Such a massive intervention immediately seized public attention and garnered huge levels of support in Quebec and Canada. By its very nature, however, it provoked much soul-searching debate and controversy. We will take up the whole question of the WMA and Pierre Trudeau's role in it later in a special section of this chapter.

On the following day, October 17, seven days after he went missing, Laporte's strangled body was found in the trunk of a car. The public was appalled. His kidnappers were subsequently sentenced for his kidnapping and murder. The kidnapping of Cross and Laporte, followed by Laporte's savage murder, had a huge impact on the minds and memory of all Quebecers and Canadians, linking terrorism forever to the month of October 1970. While these events were the climax of terrorism in Quebec, they were unique only in the selection of their high-profile victims in a new program of kidnapping and explicit political blackmail. By then, the FLQ had upped their game. Years before, terrorism with its wanton, almost mindless, bombing campaign took its toll on Quebec society and on the lives of truly innocent people.

Quebec's Troubled History of Terrorism in the 1960s

The first terrorist attack occurred on March 8, 1963, when the Royal 22nd Victoria Rifles was attacked with Molotov cocktails. With little physical damage and no one hurt, this act of terrorism seemed to point to the amateurism of the perpetrators. Yet this first bombing quite understandably attracted the public's attention to the FLQ, which was described by its members as "a revolutionary movement composed of volunteers ready to die for the economic independence of Quebec."[8] The press didn't quite know how to react to this very new kind of event. Gérard Pelletier, editor-in-chief of *La Presse,* wrote on March 12: "Should we shrug our shoulders and tell ourselves it was a ridiculous incident?" But he quickly corrected this line of thought declaring: "If the first three bombs went off like firecrackers … there is nothing to say that the next three will be equally inoffensive."[9]

Pelletier was right in suspecting that the next bombs would be more deadly. In fact, as William Tetley has written in a superb analysis of the October Crisis, "two hundred more bombings occurred between 1963 and October 1970."[10] Many of these resulted in broken lives and casualties:

- On April 21, 1963, a powerful FLQ bomb exploded in a garbage bin behind a five-storey building in downtown Montreal. The bomb killed the night watchman, Wilfrid O'Neil, who was sixty-five and due to retire the following month.[11]
- On May 17, 1963, the FLQ launched an attack on the municipality of Westmount, perceived as home to an anglophone economic elite and hence enemies of Quebec. Bombs were planted in numerous mailboxes. After a thorough search of the mailboxes, the police found many of the bombs. One of the policemen, a forty-two-year-old Polish immigrant called Walter Leja, spent five hours on the operating table after a bomb explosion. His life was saved, yet he was disabled for the rest of his life. Partially paralyzed, he could neither hear nor speak. [12]

- On August 29, 1964, Leslie MacWilliams and Alfred Pinisch, two employees of a firearms company, were killed during an FLQ robbery.
- On May 5, 1966, a bomb sent in a parcel at La Grenade shoe factory killed an employee called Thérèse Morin.
- On July 14, 1966, Jean Corbo, a sixteen-year-old member and carrier for the FLQ, was killed when the bomb he was placing blew up.
- On June 24, 1970, Jeanne d'Arc Saint-Germain, an employee at the National Defence Headquarters in Ottawa, was killed by an FLQ bomb.

The Quebec and federal governments often acted effectively against the FLQ. On May 23, 1963, Premier Jean Lesage delivered a noteworthy TV address announcing the offering of a fifty-thousand-dollar reward for information. A few days later, on May 28, thanks to a whistleblower, the attorney general was able to hold an inquest and bring charges against twenty-one suspects. Raymond Villeneuve and Gabriel Hudon, the two top leaders of the group, admitted they had stolen explosives and used bombs that killed innocent people, including O'Neil.[13] With a single dissenting vote, the jury declared that all twenty-one persons were criminally responsible for the murder of O'Neil. In a news conference, the police announced that the FLQ was no longer a public danger. Many Quebecers believed that this marked the end of the FLQ as well as the end of terrorism in Quebec. Unfortunately, this was not the case.

The inquest generated sympathy for the suspects. The RIN, *Rassemblement pour l'Indépendance Nationale* (Rally for Quebec's Independence), which had been active since September 1960, organized a public discussion led by Pierre Bourgault, who was an excellent orator. In front of hundreds of people who filled the hall, Bourgault "explained" why the violence shouldn't be attributed to the FLQ. The real culprits, he claimed, were elsewhere. The violence should be blamed, first, on the great number of Quebecers who accepted submissively the domination of their governments.[14] It was time for them to awake from their slumber, he declared, and look at their world as it really was. All the Canadian governments, supposedly composed of educated politicians, had stirred up a nationalist fervour but had done nothing to fulfill the Quebec people's aspirations. Bourgault blamed himself, as well as all other intellectuals who hadn't worked hard enough to bring about Quebec's independence.

The thunderous applause was unstoppable. At the end of this "public discussion," many hundreds of dollars were donated to support the members of the FLQ (in French, the *felquistes*). Bourgault was not alone in supporting the FLQ; dozens of intellectuals, including writers, actors, artists, and professors, signed a petition to be sent to the government's attorney general, condemning the police for what they called "a number of unjustifiable actions." It is hard to understand that the idea of a group of terrorists freely walking in the streets, seeking ways to kill or harm innocent people, didn't disturb the members of this rally. In the eyes of a good number of French Quebecers, the FLQ was a movement worthy of the people's support. This, of course, encouraged the FLQ to continue its activities and to become even more radical. In fact, within the FLQ, some of the members bemoaned the amateurism of their movement and sought more effective action.[15]

In October 1965, a group of critics within the FLQ decided to examine their movement and weren't at all happy with what they discovered. A new *felquiste*, Mathieu Hébert, who claimed to be a "convinced revolutionary," became a major contributor to *La Cognée*, the magazine of the movement. He wrote an article entitled "Does the FLQ Exist?" which claimed that the FLQ activities were purely amateurish. The FLQ, he wrote, was good at making noise rather than overthrowing the existing order: "The struggle we have undertaken is not an adventure. It is a genuine war, subject to the scientific laws of warfare."[16] By that he meant that the fundamental objectives of the FLQ shouldn't be to set bombs here and there but, far more importantly, to get rid of the capitalist system and its government. Probably under his influence, in January 1966, the journal announced the formation of the *Armée de Liberation du Québec* and issued a call to action: "Above all, *La Cognée* urges you to engage in concerted action, strikes, violent demonstrations, and, if necessary, bombs."[17] These directives led to a new bombing campaign.

The new series of bombings began on May 5, 1965, at the La Grenade shoe store, a manufacturing company owned and operated by a francophone family, in a francophone area of Montreal. This company was embroiled in a labour dispute in which the employers refused to accede to the demands of their workers. To combat such a capitalist enterprise, the FLQ decided to act. They sent a militant dressed as a messenger delivering a gift box. When he handed this box to the person who came to the door, a powerful explosion occurred. Five persons were seriously injured, and one died; two of the injured were the owners of the store, and the rest were employees. For the first time, the FLQ had targeted a company owned and run by francophone Quebecers, and all the victims were francophone. Here the struggle against capitalism was given priority over ethnicity or language.

Almost a year later, again under the influence of Mathieu Hébert, the FLQ organized an attack that once again targeted francophones, but for the first time was aimed at the political system as well. An important Quebec election was scheduled to be held on June 5, and the FLQ saw it as an occasion to strike at the politicians. Two days before the election date, during a rally in Paul Sauvé Arena with six thousand persons in attendance, the FLQ struck. As René Lévesque, then still a member of the Liberal Party, was speaking passionately, a bomb exploded in the men's washroom. However, no one was seriously hurt. The police examined the results of the bomb and dismissed it as an amateurish job. Again a fizzled attack, reinforcing the new perspective taught by Mathieu Hébert that the FLQ was failing.

On July 14, 1966, another explosion occurred behind the Dominion Textile plant in Saint-Henri, a working-class neighbourhood (in contrast with wealthy Westmount). While doing his rounds, the security guard heard a loud explosion. When the police arrived, they ran toward the car where the explosion had occurred. They found the dead body of a young man in the front seat, with his arms and right leg completely severed. This was Jean Corbo, a sixteen-year-old member of the FLQ who had been tasked with placing the bomb. His father, Nicolo Corbo, denounced the FLQ for using his son as a naive instrument of their terrorism.

The FLQ and the Quebec Intelligentsia

At this point, the police launched a search for the perpetrators of the bombings. They found and arrested several *felquistes*, who pleaded guilty to multiple offences. Almost all of them were convicted and received prison sentences. Two of the leaders of the Gang, Pierre Vallières and Charles Gagnon, as well as five others, were convicted of the manslaughter of Thérèse Morin, who died in the explosion at the La Grenade shoe store, and of the sixteen-year-old member of the FLQ, Jean Corbo, who died in the bombing at the Dominion Textile factory. Vallières received a life sentence that was later overturned and replaced by thirty months in prison. Vallières and Gagnon fled to the United States and launched a hunger strike at the United Nations headquarters in New York to protest what they claimed to be Quebec's plight in Canada. Vallières was held in a House of Detention for Men before being extradited to Canada. During his four months of detention, he wrote the famous bestseller *Nègres blancs d'Amérique*, which was translated as *White Niggers of America* and published on March 15, 1968. Many Quebec intellectuals rushed to the rescue of Vallières, Gagnon, and other members of the FLQ.

Shortly after Vallières's conviction, several singers, writers, and journalists created a *Comité d'aide au groupe Vallières-Gagnon* (Commission to Assist the Vallières-Gagnon Group). "Two members of this commission — the singer Pauline Julien and the journalist Jacques Larue-Langlois — organized an evening of solidarity called *Poèmes et chansons de la résistance*."[18] A few dozen of the leading musicians and writers, including such well-known stars as singer Robert Charlebois, actor Jean Duceppe, and poet Gaston Miron, participated. As expected, the Gesù Hall in Montreal was packed solid with a standing-room-only crowd. Similar support arose in meetings held in Hull, Sherbrooke, Trois-Rivières, and Quebec City.[19]

The FLQ mastered the kind of propaganda that appealed to young left-leaning people, and thus to teachers, academics, and, more generally, nationalists and separatists, regardless of their age. Many of these, especially the young, joined in public strikes in solidarity with the FLQ. For example, after the kidnapping of Cross, nearly one thousand students at the University of Montreal signed a petition supporting the FLQ's 1970 Manifesto, which made the following claims:

> The Front de libération du Québec wants total independence for Quebecers, united in a free society and purged for good of the clique of voracious sharks, the patronizing "big bosses" and their henchmen who have made Quebec their private hunting ground for "cheap labor" and unscrupulous exploitation.[20]

Many francophone nationalists welcomed this florid language. They believed that the FLQ was a powerful instrument for Quebec's freedom and sovereignty. In striking contrast to that dystopian world, the FLQ declared itself "the people's best friend ... representing a vast gathering of love and fraternity."[21] Yet at the same time, the FLQ would be a dreaded instrument of death for its hated enemies. Using fantastic lurid language, the Manifesto predicted:

> Soon, the English, the federalists, the lackeys of the imperialists, all those who betray the workers and Quebec's nation, will be afraid of losing their lives, and they would be right. Because soon, the FLQ will start killing.[22]

"Eminent Personalities," Modestly to the Rescue!

On October 14, 1970, at a press conference held during the crisis, a petition signed by sixteen persons was read aloud and distributed to the public and to the media. It was organized by Jacques Parizeau,[23] who claimed that Claude Ryan was the author. It was read by René Lévesque and was published the next day in *Le Devoir*. It was variously referred to as the work of "the sixteen eminent personalities," the "committee of sixteen," or "committee Lévesque/Ryan."[24] The composition of the group of signatories was as follows: one journalist, one businessman, three leaders of the Parti Québécois (PQ), four university professors, and seven union leaders, all of whom were nationalists. Claude Ryan, editor and publisher of *Le Devoir*, was the only one in this group to have recognized the legitimacy of Canadian federalism. But he was alarmed that the federal government in this crisis was manipulating Quebec and its government.

As we have seen, Ryan was in many respects ideologically very close to Lévesque, yet as leader of the Liberal Party, he would fight Lévesque and the PQ in the 1980 referendum and subsequently serve as a minister in the Bourassa government. The top three "eminent personalities" were party brass at the top of the PQ. Lévesque, of course, was the leader; Parizeau, the president of the Executive Council; and Camille Laurin, leader of the Parti Québécois caucus in the National Assembly. Most of the sixteen signatories were in varying degrees supporters of the PQ and tilted heavily toward nationalism and separatism. They advocated leniency toward the terrorist group.

René Lévesque began the press conference by asserting that "Quebec no longer has a government."[25] Jacques Parizeau explained that "it became evident in the minds of a number of people [that] if the government [fell] we would take up the slack."[26] Marcel Rioux confirmed this view and wrote: "A group of personalities ... decided to come to the aid of their government and to make a determined effort to save the lives of the two hostages."[27] Clearly, these people wanted to "aid the government," but they didn't specify the nature of this "aid." In apparent collusion with these separatist leaders, Ryan preferred that a new government be formed during the transition to support Quebec through the crisis.

The signatories of the petition asserted that the October Crisis was a matter exclusively concerning Quebec. The first sentence of the petition read as follows: "The Cross-Laporte affair is above all a Quebec drama. Of the two hostages, one is a citizen of Quebec, the other is a diplomat whose functions make him temporarily a fellow citizen." There are odd ideas in this sentence. First, it implies that one can be a "citizen of Quebec," as if Quebec were a nation-state. The objective here, of course, was to present Quebec as a legitimate nation-state, which meant that the Quebec government had the sole duty and presumably the know-how to deal with the crisis. The role of the federal government was pointedly ignored. Clearly, the objective of the petition wasn't so much directed at solving the terrorism problem but at presenting Quebec as an autonomous state: "The reputation and the collective honour of our society, the danger of social and political degeneration, makes it self-evident to us that it is Quebec which has the responsibility for finding and carrying out a solution and must put it into effect."

The petition proceeded to reject "outsiders" who endangered Quebec's honour:

> Some outside commentaries, the most recent and most incredible of which is that of Premier Robarts of Ontario, adding to the atmosphere of virtual military rigidity that can be detected in Ottawa, in our opinion threaten to reduce Quebec and its government to tragic impotence.[28]

The critique of "virtual military rigidity" here is not only addressed to Premier Robarts but also to "Ottawa," namely, the Trudeau government. Finally, the "eminent personalities" expressed their principal objective as follows: "Keeping in mind that we are vitally concerned Québécois, we wish to give our most urgent support to negotiating the exchange of the two hostages for the political prisoners."[29] The first part of the sentence implies that Bourassa is not a "vitally concerned Québécois" and therefore cannot properly negotiate. Thus, Bourassa evidently needs the help of these "sixteen eminent personalities."

From then on, the discussion of the necessity of a "provisional government" was widely discussed in the press. On October 25, 1970, the night of his election victory as mayor of Montreal, Jean Drapeau referred to various attempts to establish that "provisional government." A day later, Peter Newman, editor of the *Toronto Star*, claimed that there had been a plot to replace the Bourassa government. For a few weeks, Claude Ryan denied any talk of a "provisional government," accusing Ottawa of inventing these malicious rumours: "There is constructed in Ottawa the theory of a plot that had the purpose of evicting Bourassa from power and supplanting him by a "provisional government."[30] Then, on October 30, in answer to the multiple rumours, Ryan finally admitted in *Le Devoir* that he had discussed the issue of a provisional government on October 11 with four senior members of his staff whom he had especially summoned to his office.

To summarize the position of the "eminent petitioners":

- First, they claimed that the crisis was a matter that concerned exclusively Quebec.
- Just as important, they accepted the FLQ designation of "political prisoners" for persons who were clearly convicted criminals.
- They disparaged the Bourassa government as unable to deal with the FLQ, with Lévesque openly claiming that "there was no longer a government in Quebec."
- They floated ideas of "coalition" or "provisional" government, requiring their "eminent" participation.
- They promoted the idea that Bourassa was playing second fiddle to the government of Pierre Trudeau, agreeing to submit his government's power to that of Mr. Trudeau.

What a failing it was to confuse "political prisoners" with convicted criminals, a bias that led to a ready willingness to negotiate with terrorists. If the Quebec government had fallen into the trap of exchanging criminals for the hostages, not only would the whole system of justice have been imperilled, but terrorists would have been encouraged to keep up their criminal actions. In fact, soon after the release of the petition, several *felquistes* took an active part in circulating it widely. They quickly realized that the "eminent personalities," reflecting nationalist and sovereigntist sentiment, had handed them a valuable gift in agreeing to the FLQ terms.

The "Big Bang": The Invocation of the WMA

We come now to the heart of the matter: how did the "big bang" arise, and was it justified given the circumstances at that time? Canada was in many respects exceptional in accommodating secessionist politics in Quebec's electoral choices and in two full-scale referendums. But no country can tolerate a malignant politics that opts for violence to achieve its objectives. The FLQ celebrated itself, on the one hand, as a vast family of love and fraternity and, on the other, welcomed an orgy of killing aimed at its English-speaking enemies. This amounted to a stark declaration of war on civil society, which, on the face of it, would doubtless justify an armed state response commensurate with the risk.

But was the "big bang" War Measures Act (WMA) a "sledgehammer to crack a peanut," as NDP leader Tommy Douglas asserted? That's colourful rhetoric, but the October Crisis was by no means peanut-scale. The authorities closest to the situation in Quebec had requested emergency powers. Should the federal government have second-guessed their judgment, as Douglas implied, and turned down their request? Trudeau answered: "In the end, I had to recognize that they [Quebec politicians] were in a better position than I was to judge the urgency of the situation."[31] For Trudeau, it was already evident, from the public declaration of the "sixteen eminent personalities" and their offering of an exchange between hostages and so-called political prisoners, that there was "general disarray" in the province.[32]

In any event, there was no more limited, emergency law available on the books, a matter that Trudeau deeply regretted. He knew that the WMA was a blunt and massive law not well suited to the circumstances in Quebec, but he sought to limit its scope with specific regulations. Plans for its replacement were quickly moving forward. As a result, on October 16, just days after the invocation of the WMA, Trudeau was quick to promise a temporary and more limited emergency law that would be focused specifically on the FLQ. On November 2, that more limited legislation came before Parliament as The Public Order (Temporary Measures) Act, 1970, to replace the WMA. It sharply restricted the earlier scope of the wartime emergency law and better protected the civil liberties of Quebecers. As Justice Minister John Turner noted, there was no intention to limit dissent but "solely to [ban] the unlawful acts and the use of the unlawful means" of the FLQ.

These temporary steps to a more appropriate emergency law ultimately led to new permanent emergency legislation passed in 1988 to accommodate several kinds of emergencies in Canada up to and including outright war. It provided better safeguards for civil liberties and for express accountability of government whenever the legislation was invoked. Ironically, it was Pierre Trudeau's son, Prime Minister Justin Trudeau, who activated this Emergencies Act for the first time in February 2022, after a long occupation of the national capital, and justified the government's decision before an independent commissioner in November of that year. Herein lies a legacy of father and son embroiled in emergencies half a century apart, both of which required careful management when local authorities proved unable to deal with the situation under normal law and procedures.

Above all, critics must remember that it was not the federal government that oversaw the roundup of Quebecers under the WMA. It was the Quebec attorney general and provincial and municipal police forces who drew up and approved the final list of detainees. It was widely acknowledged that the police forces, with little intelligence on the FLQ, were realistically in no position to know how to do that effectively. The list, developed in haste, caught hundreds of perfectly innocent people in its net, a fact acknowledged by Bourassa's government. Confessing its overreach, it offered compensation to those unjustly affected. Without doubt, this deplorable lapse of judgment harmed the civil rights of many Quebecers.[33] But the fact remains that the operative government, in both the request for and administration of the WMA, lay squarely in Quebec City.

A Conversation with a Witness

On May 25, 2000, authors Monique and Max Nemni had a conversation with Marc Lalonde to better understand Trudeau's invocation of the WMA. (This interview was subsequently published in the magazine *Cité libre.*[34]) They opened the discussion by asking who it was that suggested recourse to the WMA: Bourassa or Trudeau? Marc Lalonde immediately replied that for at least ten days, Trudeau refused to use the WMA. He firmly believed that there was no need for recourse to such an extraordinary law, since there was sufficient basis in existing legislation for the police to operate. However, the authorities in both Montreal and Quebec wanted more powers and put a lot of pressure on Trudeau to pass either a special law or the WMA. Lalonde then said: "As time passed, it became evident that the police forces had begun to doubt their ability to track down the kidnappers.... There were demonstrations in support of the FLQ, including an enormous gathering of close to 5,000 people chanting 'Vive le FLQ!'"

Under those circumstances, Lalonde explained that the pressures from the provincial government and from Mayor Drapeau for emergency powers kept mounting. In response Trudeau told Lalonde:

> If Jean Drapeau's and Robert Bourassa's request is authentic as they say, they are going to have to submit it to me officially in writing. If things get too hot, I don't want them to disappear in the smoke ... and everyone will blame the Canadian government then. [Lalonde went on to say:] So I was mandated to get a letter signed by Bourassa and another signed by Drapeau.[35]

At this point, explained Lalonde, the question was transferred to the cabinet, where frequent meetings were held during all the days preceding the final decision. Obviously, opinions varied on all these questions. But finally, the cabinet concluded that a special law presented too many disadvantages: it would take too long and damage success by alerting the FLQ in advance to the government's plan. So, the cabinet decided to resort to the WMA. Lalonde concluded by emphasizing again that *Trudeau remained opposed to the WMA: "He still thought that the current legislation was adequate* [emphasis added]."

In conclusion and to summarize our findings:

- Recourse to the WMA proceeded by due process.
- The Trudeau Cabinet finally accepted the views of Bourassa and Drapeau and authorized the invocation of the WMA.
- All three levels of governments agreed that some strong means of action had to be used.
- To say that Trudeau was solely or predominantly responsible is both simplistic and wrong.

Lalonde also reminded us of the reactions of the people when Bourassa and Drapeau signed the letters: "The great majority of Canadians were behind their governments!... Look at the surveys of the day; look at the vote in the House: It was something like 190 votes to 16. The support was huge!" Polls certainly made that point clear. For example, the Gallup Poll of December 12, 1970, showed that 89 percent of English Canadians and 86 percent of French-speaking Canadians approved of the government actions.

While students had always been more inclined to protest in favour of the FLQ and the "Revolution," their position changed quickly, as Eric Bédard wrote in his analysis of the October Crisis in the universities and CEGEPs: "The shock caused by the death of Pierre Laporte and the WMA was the last nail in the Revolution's coffin." Similarly, most members of trade unions, in opposition to their anti-WMA leaders, supported the use of the War Measures Act. So too did the business community, which declared on October 23: "Le conseil du patronat du Québec (CPQ) wishes it to be known publicly that it gives full support to the Quebec government as concerns the difficult decisions that it was called upon to make during the events of the last few days."[36]

It was Frank Scott, eminent law professor at McGill University, who set out the essential distinction between separatism pursued through legitimate politics and the politics of violence:

> The legitimate activities of the Parti Québécois which aims to prove through democratic means that a majority in Quebec are in favour of independence is not in question now. This party has existed for some years now, it is distinct from the FLQ....
>
> It is not separatism in Quebec that is outlawed, it is a ... revolutionary movement applying new techniques of terror.[37]

The Aftermath of the Big Bang

Ironically, as the crisis receded into history, sentiment around the use of the WMA shifted from overwhelming support to almost mainstream criticism. In part, this was a natural reaction to the detaining of hundreds of innocent people who were unjustly incarcerated by the Quebec police and to the sheer scale of the WMA. Though most of these were released within a week, the plight of these detainees was taken up in countless nationalist critiques. Many of the principal figures during the crisis — PQ and labour leaders, intellectuals — have remained silent or offered different accounts of their roles during these events.[38] Many who had originally supported the measure also began to have second thoughts. But others, like noted historian J.L. Granatstein, went in the other direction. At first a critic of the use of the WMA, despite hostility from his students, he later acknowledged, in a chapter entitled "Changed Positions," his later acceptance, marvelling at the rapid shift of public opinion to a more critical stance.[39]

Of course, it is to be expected that opinion during crisis will often differ from judgment in later quieter times. History too will reflect changing perspectives, always seeking to have the last word on the past. But the judgment of statesmen in any actual emergency must consider the choices available under the prevailing circumstances. And even more importantly, judgment must look to the *actual outcome* of government actions on the country. By these standards, Canada came through the crisis reasonably well.

Certainly, that was the opinion of Prime Minister Pierre Trudeau, responsible for managing the crisis at the federal level and making the decision whether to negotiate with terrorists or to fight back. In his address to the nation announcing the WMA, he gave his forthright answer to the FLQ:

> To bow to the pressures of these kidnappers who demand that the prisoners be released would be not only an abdication of responsibility, it would lead to an increase in terrorist activities in Quebec. It would be as well an invitation to terrorism and kidnapping across the country.
>
> If a democratic society is to continue to exist, it must be able to root out the cancer of an armed revolutionary movement that is bent on destroying the very basis of our freedom.[40]

More than two decades after the events, Trudeau in his *Memoirs* stressed the need for a political leader to manage a crisis when it arises or lose control of the situation. Above all, there can be no compromise with armed criminals: "The first duty of government is to govern: which means never giving in to chaos or terror." He continued: "As for the long-term effects of the October Crisis and the methods we used to bring it to an end, they seem to have shut down the activities of the FLQ for good, which is no small thing."[41]

SIX

"Welcome to the 1980s"

WITH THESE JUBILANT WORDS, DECLARED ON THE EVE OF HIS ELECTION TRIUMPH ON February 18, 1980, Pierre Trudeau proudly announced his political resurrection. Just nine months after losing an election on May 22, 1979, and just eighty-nine days after formally resigning as Liberal leader and from active political office on November 21, 1979, Trudeau was back. One might even say, "back with a vengeance."

Yes, a life in politics could be enthralling, but it was also no rose garden. Trudeau was painfully aware that he had had to sacrifice his private life for public service on numerous occasions. He had resisted the pressures to run for the 1968 leadership to replace Lester Pearson to protect "my sacrosanct personal freedom," to avoid his life being swallowed up by public office, so that his life no longer belonged to himself.[1] Yet this was the burden of the statesman, and he paid the price for it repeatedly. After those initial sunny days of Trudeaumania came a decade of crises — the invoking of the WMA, growing Quebec separatism, exploding energy prices, stagflation with wage- and price-control legislation. These had all taken their toll. Even worse, from his personal perspective, was the unravelling in the mid-70s of the Trudeau marriage in the full glare of public life; moreover, the children of that broken marriage needed their father. There were many reasons why Pierre Trudeau would have welcomed the lifting of that public burden and a return to private life.

Yet he constantly "vacillated between going and staying."[2] Scarcely weeks after making the decision to retire from political office, he was tempted again to sacrifice his private life for that of the statesman. Crafty Liberal plotters, like House Leader Allan MacEachen, were inviting him back as leader, luring him into a plan to defeat Joe Clark's first budget and bring down his minority government. The caucus, the party executive, and many of his friends joined the chorus. How could he resist? It had been galling for Trudeau to read the political obituaries, to learn what the pundits thought of his flawed record, his ambition "unfulfilled." Yet Trudeau had to admit that the chief objects of his statesmanship — securing patriation of the Constitution, an amending formula for making changes to the Constitution and a Charter of Rights and Freedoms —had not been achieved. His task was not yet done.

Looking back, Trudeau lamented that the 1971 Victoria constitutional conference, named in honour of this charming city on Vancouver Island, had come "within a hair's breadth of success," failing only because "Premier Robert Bourassa was not strong enough to keep his commitments." He went on:

> I don't believe in fretting too much about historical-might-have-beens. But if we had succeeded at Victoria, Quebec would have achieved its dream of obtaining a constitutional veto, language rights would have been promoted across the country, and the country would have been spared a decade of constitutional wrangling.[3]

This musing through rose-tinted glasses surely underestimates the forces driving Canada's constitutional politics — above all, Quebec's continuing demand for special status or independence and Western Canada's demand "to be let in." Yet it's worth remembering the remarkable moment that was Victoria 1971, when unanimity was achieved on a balanced package of constitutional reforms including:

- patriation, the final bringing home, renaming, and "patriating" of the Canadian Constitution (still called the British North America Act) from the U.K. Parliament;

- an agreed domestic amending formula for Canadians to make changes to their Constitution in their own country (no longer a colony requesting changes to our Constitution by a mother country's Parliament);
- a modest Charter of Rights written into our Constitution, protecting basic civil liberties, such as freedom of speech, assembly, and protection from discrimination; and
- reform of our Constitution's division of powers between governments by removing certain outdated federal powers and modestly increasing provincial powers.

Yes, this was a fondly remembered moment in time. But that was then; this was now. The sun was rising on the 1980s. The fight for the hearts and minds of Quebecers lay only a few months ahead with the approaching Quebec referendum on sovereignty-association. He could not step away. It would be a tumultuous four years later before Pierre Trudeau would finally take his "walk in the snow" and leave office for good.

The 1980 Quebec referendum drew Trudeau into the fray only on a few major occasions, provoking his vintage scorn and passion. The most dramatic of these was at the Paul Sauvé Arena on May 14, just six days before the referendum vote. There he scorned the PQ government's muddled referendum question asking consent "to negotiate a new agreement with the rest of Canada based on the equality of nations, to acquire Quebec sovereignty, and at the same time to maintain with Canada an economic association including a common currency." Trudeau pointed out that the question cowardly avoided a straight up "yes" or "no" vote on leaving Canada, and which, even if successful with a "yes" vote, was a "dead end," as it neither authorized governments outside Quebec to negotiate "sovereignty-association" nor justified Quebec independence.

But his fury with the PQ in that speech reached boiling point when he attacked what he saw as their disgusting efforts to dismiss his identity as a Quebecer by harping on his middle name "Elliott," suggesting he was, by that measure, not a "true" Quebecer:

> Mon nom est Québécois [he said in a play on words of the "No" campaign slogan, "Mon non est Québécois"].
>
> But my name is a Canadian name also, and that's the story of my name.
>
> Now I ask you, is Johnson [Pierre Marc Johnson and his father and brother Daniel] an English name or a French name?... [What about Péquistes — members or supporters of the PQ] with names like "Louis O'Neill and Robert Burns"?[4]

His denunciation of this cynical PQ attempt to divide Quebecers by name sent the packed arena into thunderous applause. Such PQ contempt was inflicted on women too, who generally leaned more to the "no" side, especially when they found themselves arrogantly painted as docile, subservient "Yvettes" by the status of women minister, Lise Payette. "Yvette" had long been pictured in Quebec textbooks as the very image of an obedient, passive girl. Payette had even gone so far as to paint Claude Ryan's activist wife, Madeleine, as an Yvette. Such divisive tactics backfired spectacularly, setting off proud women's Yvette rallies throughout the province, expanding instead of narrowing the gender gap.

Trudeau's speech was equally fierce on what a "no" vote would mean. He demanded Canadian constitutional reform. In striking contrast to his politics in all the foregoing years, this time would be different:

> I can make a most solemn commitment that following a NO vote, we will immediately take action to renew the Constitution and we will not stop until we have done that.
>
> And I make a solemn declaration to all Canadians in the other provinces, we, the Québec MPs, are laying ourselves on the line, because we are telling Quebecers to vote NO and telling you in the other provinces that we will not agree to your interpreting a NO vote as an indication that everything is fine and can remain as it was before.
>
> We want change and we are willing to lay our seats in the House on the line to have change.

This was a staggering declaration, announcing his shared alignment with virtually all Quebec MPs in the conviction that the time for decisive action had come. Quebecers' votes for a reformed Canada would be honoured and would not be stopped. This was a warning to all provincial premiers that Ottawa would proceed unilaterally to amend the Constitution, on its own, if necessary. This was the beginning of constitutional hard ball.

Change by Agreement vs Acting Alone?

Following his success in winning virtually 60 percent of the referendum vote, Trudeau called the premiers together on June 9 in one last attempt to secure agreement in the federal-provincial negotiations over the summer. A First Ministers Conference was scheduled for September to see whether an agreement had been or could be reached. And if not, Trudeau announced that his government would proceed to act alone in taking forward a package of constitutional changes to the Westminster Parliament. The choice for leaders and country then was clear: change through a federal-provincial agreement or through unilateral federal action.

The premiers — not a single Liberal among them — were not amused. Nor did they panic at this threat. With the federal win in the Quebec referendum, the premiers reverted to form, demanding a long list of increased provincial powers as the price to be paid for patriation of the Constitution.

Plus ça change, plus c'est la même chose.

No, not this time, Trudeau resolved. No concession to "blackmail." No holdup of the constitutional train. No "giving away the store," as he felt he had done in his 1978–79 offer. While an ambitious agenda consisting of no less than twelve constitutional issues was agreed upon, this time, unlike the past, there was an alternative route to patriation: Ottawa acting alone. After securing and then losing agreement at Victoria in 1971, Trudeau had threatened the premiers with unilateral action as early as 1976. This time — after his political resurrection and solemn promises in the Quebec referendum — this time, by God, he would do it.

While this threat hung over the summer 1980 negotiations, it did not change the substance or direction of the talks. Provinces that had proposed items dear to their hearts — increased powers over natural resources for the Western provinces, for example, or increased power over offshore resources for Newfoundland — continued to press these claims with considerable success. Despite the risk, the bargaining strategy of most premiers was to support each other's positions in a growing provincialist ganging up on Ottawa.[5] As Trudeau acidly put it: "They [the other premiers] had enrolled in the school of blackmail, of which Quebec was the founder and top-ranking graduate."[6]

The PQ government, indeed, quietly encouraged that strategy and sought to build a broad provincial alliance against the federal government as its best way of ensuring the failure of the conference. It was understood by virtually all participants that the PQ government was unwilling to be a party to successful federal reform, yet nevertheless it was expected to negotiate in good faith. Such was the odd position of a PQ government that had lost its separatist mandate in the May 1980 referendum and was obliged instead to participate in federal-provincial constitutional renewal. But clearly its heart was not in it. Their best deal for the future of sovereignty-association was "no deal."

From the perspective of the federal government, the most disappointing part of the negotiations was the overwhelming provincial opposition to the Charter that formed the heart of what Ottawa called its "People's Package." While Ontario, New Brunswick, and Newfoundland supported an entrenched Charter and Saskatchewan supported only language rights, the rest of the provinces objected vigorously to the principle and substance of an entrenched bill of rights. They argued that such a change would take Canada away from its venerable tradition of parliamentary sovereignty, inherited from the mother country, the U.K., and move it toward a U.S. republican model. As Sterling Lyon, then premier of Manitoba, strenuously argued, rights were at least as well protected in countries with parliamentary systems of government as they were in countries like the U.S., with legalistic systems of rights, entrenched in the Constitution but often inadequately defended by courts. This was an old debate, perhaps even a sentimental one, that now took centre stage in September before an immense audience on Canadian national television. There was no knockout punch — not least because both systems had their virtues and vices. But there was no doubt that the proposed Charter would graft an American-style legal system onto Canada's Constitution and expand accordingly the importance of the judicial branch of government for the protection of Canadians' rights and freedoms.

For the Canadian public, the rhetorical advantage lay with Pierre Elliott Trudeau. Why would a people not welcome a new rights Charter as a check on and addition to their parliamentary system of government? Yet the debate widened the gulf among governments, leaving them in a stalemate, edging them ever closer to a very tough fight over unilateral patriation, namely, Trudeau's threat of "going it alone" to the Westminster Parliament. Why were all the parties taking this risk? It had been assumed that Trudeau was using that threat of unilateral patriation primarily as a bargaining lever and that he would be reluctant to take the risk of going to the Westminster Parliament without substantial provincial consent.

Yet on the eve of the First Ministers Conference that September, the leak of the secret Kirby Memorandum to Cabinet, authored by Michael Kirby, then secretary to the cabinet for federal-provincial relations, made clear to the premiers that planning for "going it alone" was real and well advanced.[7] In fact, this document showed Ottawa's uncanny grasp of the profound political and legal issues likely to be faced by unilateral patriation in both the courts and the country. Yet, despite the acknowledged risks of defying constitutional convention, the spirit of this memorandum was feisty and hawkish, reflecting the confidence of the government after its win in the Quebec referendum.

In fact, Pierre Elliott Trudeau had been thinking about the possibility of unilateral patriation for at least three decades before 1980. He had witnessed the failed attempt at patriation as a young man during his brief stint working under Gordon Robertson in the PCO in Ottawa in 1949–51. Even then, the blocking of patriation disturbed and obsessed him. He started to ponder at that point whether unilateral patriation might become necessary if the provinces continued to obstruct what he felt to be an essential step in Canadian nationhood. Remarkably, this very scenario had even been presciently suggested in a book Trudeau was then reviewing at the author's request. Would a time come, Paul Gérin-Lajoie mused in *Constitutional*

Amendment in Canada (1950), when federal action would seriously seek "to abridge provincial sovereignty without the consent of the affected provinces?" He continued: "Yet this contention [federal unilateralism] might result some day — a day which may be not far distant — in creating a trend of opinion which would make its way openly into the federal Cabinet and would finally gain the support of a majority in Parliament."[8] Ironically, Trudeau, the young scholar, would, thirty years later, as prime minister, put that question to the test.

On September 8, Trudeau was presented with the "Château consensus," drafted by Quebec and approved by the premiers over breakfast at the Château Laurier. In Trudeau's words, this "demanded ten powers in exchange for discussing patriation and then another twelve before the deed was done." Snorting his disapproval, he declared:

> Well now we know there will never be an agreement. You guys are laughing at me — you're going back to square one. But I'm telling you gentlemen, I've been warning you since 1976 that we could introduce a resolution in the House of Commons patriating the constitution, and if necessary, we'll do this unilaterally. So I'm telling you now, we're going to go it alone. We're going to introduce a resolution, and we'll go to London, and we won't even bother asking a premier to come with us.[9]

Trudeau had thrown down the gauntlet. Thus began the mightiest of federal-provincial constitutional battles in Canada's history. But despite Trudeau's boast, he sought continuously whatever provincial consent to his resolution that he could find. First, he sought it with Premier Davis of Ontario and Premier Hatfield of New Brunswick, who had supported the Charter during the summer negotiations, and then, in secret negotiations, with Premier Blakeney of Saskatchewan over several months. The first two, Premiers Davis and Hatfield, announced at once their support for the federal initiative, while Premier Blakeney equivocated, finally deciding instead to join with the dissenting premiers in what became known as the Gang of Eight.

In fact, Trudeau had carefully prepared the ground for patriation. He had raised the matter with British prime minister Margaret Thatcher in June 1980 and received her assurances that "if the Parliament of Canada asked for its constitution, there was nothing her Parliament could do but to accede to that request."[10] He had laid plans to isolate the opposition to the Conservatives in the Canadian Parliament by securing the approval of the NDP leader, Ed Broadbent, prior to his television announcement of unilateral patriation on October 2. This was a remarkable coup, appearing to bring onside thirty-two NDP members of Parliament, twenty-seven of whom represented Western Canada. In return, Trudeau promised to include increased provincial powers over natural resources in the resolution. Broadbent anticipated that this promise would bring in Premier Blakeney to support the measure, aligning the NDP federally and provincially. This proved to be a vain hope. The party would remain deeply torn over the whole unilateral patriation process.

"Torn" is an apposite word to describe widespread reaction to unilateral patriation in Canada. On the one hand, the Charter was hugely popular among the Canadian public, while, on the other, there was considerable wariness over the process that was dividing the country. The Kirby Memorandum had anticipated that opposition would focus on the process and had urged that the resolution be approved swiftly by Parliament before the end of the year, preferably before the results of any court challenges to it. That objective proved elusive, as courts of appeal in three provinces — Manitoba, Newfoundland, and Quebec — began at once to consider "direct reference questions,"* asking whether the federal resolution was both lawful and consistent with Canada's constitutional conventions. Such questions would invariably draw the courts into the very heart of the country's politics. And the courts' judgments would themselves shape the outcome of the constitutional battle being waged.

It took just a few months for provincial courts to issue their judgments — federal victories in Manitoba (three justices to two) and Quebec (four

* Reference questions are those that provinces can put to their Courts of Appeal or that the federal government can put directly to the Supreme Court asking for an official opinion on questions of law or convention. Provincial reference case judgments could in turn be appealed to the Supreme Court for a final judgment.

justices to one), with the Newfoundland Court unanimously declaring on March 31, 1981, that the federal resolution was illegal. After that, there was no avoiding a Supreme Court review, with hearings scheduled a mere week after Parliament had approved all amendments to the resolution on April 23, 1981.

The Public Acts to Strengthen the Charter

Thanks to the extraordinary interest and participation of the public in pressing for changes at the parliamentary committee level, rights and freedoms in the Charter were enhanced and much better secured. While it made for a delay in the proceedings, this groundswell of public support for a strong Charter strengthened the hand of Ottawa and weakened that of the opposing provinces. More importantly, the amendments made Canada's emerging Charter one of the strongest of its kind in the world. Moreover, this process of what was called "constitutionalizing charter Canadians" as participants and recipients of constitutional reform had begun, fostering Canadians' understanding that the Constitution of Canada belonged to them.[11]

This happy outcome was largely due to the exceedingly fine work of the Special Joint Committee on the Constitution. Its all-party members managed to focus on the substance of the Constitution and engage with the public in a thorough and thoughtful review. In this way, in the committee's words, "the public became the author of its own history, [where] the voices of hundreds of individuals and organizations representing an extraordinarily diverse cross-section of Canadian society" could be heard:

> For the first time in Canadian history, television shined the spotlight on a committee's work and captured the attention of the nation. The engagement of the broader public, combined with the ideas and passions of the witnesses who spoke to the Committee, softened a process that would otherwise have been partisan, and the end result was a stronger Charter of Rights.[12]

As Deputy Minister of Justice Roger Tassé noted, this "intense public scrutiny breathed new life into the patriation debate and changed the terms of the debate from the oft-inaccessible subject of federalism to the comprehensible and popular one of human rights."[13] Of course, this was the principal objective of Pierre Trudeau: to make the Constitution a matter of individual rights and not just of governments and collective communities. That was the reason for calling the Charter an essential part of the "People's Package." Hence, when Trudeau and the whole Liberal caucus saw that the committee's work was strengthening the Charter and building public support behind it, they granted it more time for its deliberations. The result was a host of amendments, approved on April 23, 1981, that improved the overall package of changes, particularly Charter rights and freedoms.[14]

The committee also offered a golden opportunity for advocates of Indigenous Rights to have their voices heard. Some thirty-seven intervenors did so, including Indigenous organizations. Intense lobbying also proceeded in Canadian capitals and in London. There were compelling reasons to do so because the federal resolution had provided no new Indigenous Rights or, for that matter, no recognition at all, but only a promise of a constitutional conference dealing with their issues after patriation. This was intolerable, leaving the rights of Indigenous Peoples in limbo. The NDP leader, Ed Broadbent, began to warn that its support depended on securing Indigenous Rights. An agreement was reached on January 30, 1981, with all the Indigenous organizations to include a new section of the Charter "recognizing and affirming Aboriginal and treaty rights."[15] Entrenching these rights in the heart of the Constitution and ensuring a constitutional conference on Indigenous matters within the following year were major stepping stones. They moved the agenda of Indigenous Peoples forward decisively from the debates of the late 1960s discussed in chapter four.

You Gotta Do the "Two-Step" at the Federal Ball

You'd have thought that these rights, in a strengthened Charter, would have won acceptance as additions to the Constitution the minute the national Parliament approved them. In many countries with a unitary top-down system of government — like France's or the U.K.'s — the agreement of the national authorities in the capital is all that is needed to make constitutional changes applicable to the whole country. But matters are not that simple in binary, non-unitary systems of government. In a country like Canada that has two authorized levels of government — a national Parliament and ten provincial legislatures — constitutional amendments that affect their respective powers need the consent of both levels of government. This is a principle that has been reflected in all proposed amending formulas in Canada's history: constitutional changes affecting both levels of government need the consent not only of the federal Parliament but also of a majority of provincial legislatures representing a majority of the Canadian population.

We could call this the federal two-step ballroom rule, the "Canadian way" of making constitutional changes. There's a similar legal rule in other federal countries for changing the Constitution: in the United States, for example, changes to the Constitution require two-thirds consent of the Houses of Congress, plus the consent of three-quarters of the American state legislatures or state conventions. In other words, getting changes made to the Constitution in federal countries like Canada is hard. The bar is set high, requiring substantial consent from two levels of government. In effect, two partners — federal and most provincial dancers — need to do the two-step in perfect unison.

An expert on federalism like Pierre Trudeau knew all this, but he also knew that until Canada put in place its own legal amendment rules, incorporating this widespread understanding, it was possible for the Canadian Parliament to bypass the provinces and go to London with a resolution requesting changes on its own. That's exactly what he was proposing to do. Pierre would dance solo, or at best lock arms with just two obliging provincial premiers, Richard Hatfield of New Brunswick and Bill Davis of Ontario. Was such a ballroom performance anything near good enough?

With no legal amendment rules in Canada's Constitution ever agreed upon, our country continued to rely upon its former imperial master in London to make changes to Canada's Constitution at Ottawa's request.[16]

Such requests took the form of a resolution passed in the Canadian Parliament and then submitted to the Queen and to the Westminster Parliament. When these requests proceeded with prior agreement and without political fanfare in Canada, there appeared to be no problem with the passing of Canadian constitutional amendments over many years. Yet Canada lacked full legal maturity, namely, the power to make changes to its own Constitution, simply by virtue of the country's failure to agree on a domestic amending formula. Hence, the call for "patriation" of the Constitution, a subject dear to the prime minister's heart; indeed, one of his advisors thought it not merely an "obsession" for Pierre Trudeau but a matter on which he was "monomaniacal."[17] Yet the road to full legal maturity and to an entrenched bill of rights depended on dancing the two-step with most premiers. Unilateral action with few or no provincial partners just wouldn't pass convention on the ballroom dance floor.

Indeed, the bare facts of unilateral patriation revealed a core discrepancy. The resolution purported to bring home the Constitution with substantial amendments affecting the powers of the provinces at the request of the Canadian Parliament with little or no provincial consent, yet all future general amendments thereafter would require the consent of every region of Canada. This time, the Canadian Parliament acting alone would use the old imperial machinery one last time to make massive changes to the Constitution, while strict federalism rules of consent would only apply later. How could this contradiction be solved?

The short answer is that it cannot be. In his *Memoirs*, Trudeau admitted that he had decided after 1980 to give up on "co-operative federalism" and to bypass normal federalism rules:

> You've got to do it alone, otherwise it will never be done. Take patriation of the constitution, for example. Every Prime Minister since 1927, since Mackenzie King, had tried to patriate with the consent of the provinces and no one had ever succeeded. I said, "It's obvious we'll never have a constitution of our own if we don't do it alone.[18]

Here, set out boldly in his own words, lies the blunt answer to the contradiction. Trudeau revealed even more of the meaning and spirit of his last term in office when he admitted that unilateralism would extend from the constitutional area to energy and economic policy areas too:

> And it was the same thing with energy [National Energy Program], and the same thing with the economy [National Industrial Policy]. That was the spirit after 1980. [To reject] the ponderous, careful pace of cooperation [and instead] just set out to get some things done.[19]

These statements are of immense importance. When warned by Premier Sterling Lyon of Manitoba that his unilateralism will "tear the country apart," Trudeau responded that "if there was not the will in the country to be constitutionally independent 115 years after Canada stopped being a colony, that would have meant that there is no national will at all, and therefore no country worthy of the name."[20] Looking back, it was exactly such federal impatience that Paul Gérin-Lajoie long ago had feared and had prophesied might arise in Ottawa. Pierre Trudeau had decided to cast off the rules and trappings of co-operative federalism and test how far Ottawa could go acting alone. The circumstances were about as propitious as could be imagined: an implacable, determined prime minister, a party heavily composed of Quebec federalists ready to put their seats on the line, and a Canadian public long impatient for constitutional resolution. Yet a powerful institution — the Supreme Court of Canada — stood in the way. It would be the courts of Canada, not its legislatures or its prime minister, that would make the crucial judgment on federal unilateralism.

Meanwhile, the Gang of Eight,* those provinces opposing Ottawa's unilateral plan with several Court challenges, finalized their own positions in mid-April 1981, at about the same time as the Canadian Parliament finalized its resolution for submission to the Queen and Parliament at Westminster.

* There were initially six provinces (Newfoundland/Labrador, P.E.I., Quebec, Manitoba, Alberta, and B.C.) who joined together as a gang, which became the Gang of Eight when Saskatchewan and Nova Scotia joined some months later.

The Gang was an uneasy alliance, not least because it comprised the premiers of seven largely English-speaking provinces alongside the recently re-elected premier René Lévesque, the avowed separatist leader of the sole majority francophone province of Quebec. How was trust to be established among them? Apart from sheer and shared opposition to Pierre Trudeau, how could a common agenda be developed? The effective leader of the English-speaking group was Peter Lougheed, premier of Alberta, who was also the man in whom Lévesque had the most confidence. Their bond helped to create and manage trust across the chasm of incompatible provincial agendas.

The first challenge for the Gang was to come up with an alternative amending formula to Trudeau's, the one that had guaranteed a veto for Quebec (and Ontario). The right to a veto had become a bottom line for Quebec governments, yet Lévesque found himself under pressure to agree to an amending formula proposed by Alberta that gave no veto to any province. In a fateful step, Lévesque agreed to Alberta's proposal, ceding the idea of a Quebec veto in return for the right of any province to opt out of amendments with the guarantee of financial compensation. This was a logical option for a separatist, since it guaranteed that Quebec could opt out of any amendments that gave provincial powers to Ottawa and still be guaranteed the funds to run its own program in any given area. Yet it was by no means an equivalent power to a veto. While Lévesque's compromise preserved the common front of the Gang, it exposed Quebec to great risk of losing for good its claim to a veto. Trudeau heaped scorn on this blunder, mocking Lévesque entering the Gang's deal-making room for having "left the veto at the door with his galoshes."[21]

While the battle for public opinion was being waged vigorously in Canada over the following months, together with intense lobbying of the British government and Parliament, the federal resolution itself remained stalled from late April 1981, pending a decision of the Supreme Court of Canada. The constitutional train, stopped in its unilateral tracks, was forced to await judicial review of its status as law and its compatibility with the country's constitutional conventions.

Trudeau Faces Judgment Day

It was the moment of truth, September 28, 1981, when the judgment of the Supreme Court was released. As a lawyer with expertise in constitutional law, and not least as the principal author of unilateral patriation, Pierre Trudeau was intensely preoccupied with what the Court would have to say on the central questions put before it. He had himself appointed many of the justices, including Chief Justice Bora Laskin, whose opinion on the questions closely conformed to his own. As it turned out, the chief justice found himself in a 7–2 majority of the Court affirming the legality of the federal resolution, but in the minority dissenting from the Court's 3–6 majority decision that it violated constitutional convention.

The Supreme Court's recognition of the nature and importance of conventions ensuring "that the legal framework of the Constitution will be operated in accordance with the prevailing constitutional values or principles" was, the Court argued, a vital and fundamental part of the total Constitution. The majority decision gave sanction to any violation of an important convention by declaring it "unconstitutional." Such a declaration would have no legal consequence, but its moral and political impact would be considerable. Coming to the heart of the matter, in a ringing declaration, the majority concluded that unilateral action was inconsistent with the federal nature of Canada:

> The federal principle cannot be reconciled with a state of affairs where the modification of provincial legislative powers could be obtained by the unilateral action of the federal authorities. It would indeed offend the federal principle that "a radical change to the constitution be taken at the request of a bare majority of the members of the Canadian House of Commons and Senate."
>
> The purpose of this conventional rule is to protect the federal character of the Canadian Constitution and prevent the anomaly that the House of Commons and Senate could obtain by simple resolution what they could not validly accomplish by statute.[22]

For Trudeau this was "a faulty judgment." No doubt angered by the Court's rebuke, his lawyerly dismissal of the federal convention was nonetheless a surprising position for a scholar and champion of federalism like himself to take.[23] Holding back his disdain for the decision while in office, he later lacerated the Court in a speech on the opening of the Bora Laskin Library in 1991 and in the presence of the then chief justice Brian Dickson. He, typically, didn't mince his words:

> [Laskin's dissent] was not only the better law, but the better common sense, and consequently it was also wiser politically. Had it prevailed over the majority view, I believe that Canada's future would have been more assured.[24]

Nevertheless, when confronted as prime minister with the Court judgment at the time, he coolly assessed the situation and drew the appropriate political response:

> As a lawyer, a teacher of constitutional law, and a former minister of justice, I felt that if the court said what we were doing was legal, we should go ahead and do it. But as a politician, [proceeding in apparent violation of constitutional convention might appear] reckless.[25]

Noting that pushing ahead without trying again to secure substantial provincial consent might undermine opinion in Canada, diminish the chances of a smooth British Parliament passage of the resolution, and jeopardize the support of the premiers of Ontario and New Brunswick, Trudeau the politician decided to give it one last try.

The story of the final November 1981 showdown between Trudeau and the Gang of Eight has become so legendary as to be apocryphal. So much lay hidden, so many stories were told, and there was so much vitriol and jubilation afterward. Under the circumstances, could it really have been otherwise? After all, not all the participants could be winners, especially when not all actually wanted a successful negotiated outcome. Trudeau was convinced that Lévesque and his separatist government would never agree to a deal. To achieve success at the negotiating table, therefore, he knew that he would have to break the Gang. Trudeau set out the stark scenario:

> When the final conference began on Monday, November 2, I knew the Eight were feeling very confident, perhaps even cocky, because of the Supreme Court's decision. I was aiming at one of two outcomes: I could either prove that the Eight were being completely unreasonable and then go ahead alone, legally but perhaps unconventionally. Or I could break the solidarity among the Eight and go to London with the support of a substantial number of premiers, which I supposed would be anywhere between five and nine of them. Lévesque's goal was to keep the Gang intact to thwart me, and mine was to make a certain number of concessions that would split their ranks and bring some of the others on side.[26]

It was on the third day that participants began to move away from reciting fixed positions. Premier Blakeney of Saskatchewan, whom Lévesque deeply distrusted, gave notice to the Gang of Eight of advancing its own separate proposal, which, according to Quebec's intergovernmental minister Claude Morin, caused "consternation" in the Quebec delegation. Though the proposal went nowhere, it was the beginning of the departure from the Gang's "common front" principles. British Columbia also announced on Wednesday morning that it would accept the entrenchment of minority language educational rights. The dreaded breakup of the Gang seemed to hang dangerously in the balance.

Lévesque Trapped by a Referendum Offer

Trudeau recognized that Quebec representatives were doubtless worrying about how far they could count on Gang unity in the face of compromises from premiers wanting a deal, and he took note of the fact that Lévesque had already announced that he might soon leave the conference. That was when the prime minister suddenly played his referendum card. It was simple and shiny — a fishing lure and hook. Turning to Lévesque, Trudeau said:

> Rather than break up in disarray and continue our fight on the doorsteps of the British Parliament, why don't we get patriation first — nobody can object to that — then give ourselves two years to solve our problems over the amending formula and the charter, and failing that, consult the people in a referendum? Surely a great democrat like yourself won't be against a referendum?
>
> Lévesque rose to the bait. I think he answered instinctively, without remembering that he was in the Gang of Eight, and said: "Well, I can buy that."
>
> I seized the moment and said to the other premiers, particularly the rest of the Gang of Eight: "This is a triumph. There is a Quebec-Ottawa alliance. You are all surprised, gentlemen. Too bad for you."[27]

Having snagged René Lévesque's agreement, and created wider consternation within the Gang of Eight, Trudeau went off happily to lunch. Without even a smirk on his face, he announced to the nation a new "Quebec-Canada alliance." Teasing the media, Trudeau quipped: "The cat is among the pigeons."[28]

The beauty of the referendum card, Trudeau's joker in the deck, was that it would work equally well as a fallback position in the event of a negotiation stalemate or of British government hesitation to pass the unilateral resolution. At the same time, it turned out to be a brilliant strategy to break up the Gang, were any premier foolish enough to accept it. Having done so, Lévesque later complained that it was a wicked trap that Trudeau had laid for him; yet, he had walked right into it. He hadn't even given Gang leaders notice of his bolting from their midst. While a referendum, if ratified, would provide undoubted legitimacy to the new Constitution, it would force all Gang premiers and governments to fight against the popular Charter of Rights and Freedoms right in their backyards. While Lévesque was confident he could win such a referendum, it was anathema to the others.

The trap was set, and the deed was done. "One could feel Trudeau literally rejoicing," complained a defeated Lévesque later. "He had put one over on us."[29] Lévesque could no longer keep the Gang intact and opposed. In fact, he lost credibility within the Gang and had ceded consent to a Charter referendum battle in the country if the federal resolution were at any stage blocked. These were conditions that favoured compromise for all the other participants if they were to avoid the international spectacle of an embarrassing Canadian brawl in London before the British government and Parliament. The elements of a compromise were put together that very night, the apocryphal "nuit des longs couteaux," or "Night of the Long Knives."

Betrayed! Raped! Abandoned! Quebec "stabbed in the back" as its delegation slept in their beds across the river in Hull! The metaphors and the narrative were riveting. Of course, Quebecers would draw their own conclusion according to their inclinations, yet how could this contest between their champions, Pierre Trudeau, the federalist, and René Lévesque, the separatist, both repeatedly winning the hearts of Quebecers with completely divergent visions for their Quebec homeland, be settled? Sad, but inevitable: what, other than a zero-sum outcome, could Quebecers seriously expect? They themselves had placed the two in power and bid them fight. Trudeau acknowledged the winner-take-all situation: "It was a matter of two totally conflicting visions of Canada and Quebec fighting it out."[30] More broadly, it reflected a profound ambivalence at the core of Quebecers' complicated feelings of identity toward Quebec and Canada.

The compromise deal was quickly sketched out on a napkin in a small kitchen on the fifth floor of the conference centre by the old trio of friends: Saskatchewan's Roy Romanow, Jean Chrétien, and Roy McMurtry, attorney general of Ontario. It was, in effect, a mutual swap over the two major items in the constitutional talks, each modified to encourage compromise:

- acceptance of the Alberta amending formula, with the deletion of financial compensation for any province opting out of amendments; and
- acceptance of the Charter of Rights and Freedoms, subject to a notwithstanding clause that would allow federal

or provincial legislatures to override court rulings against their legislation.

Trudeau was not ready to accept this deal. He reversed himself that Wednesday night only after Premier Bill Davis informed him by phone that neither Ontario nor New Brunswick would continue to support unilateral patriation unless he went along with this emerging compromise. During that long night, British Columbia and Alberta premiers pressed and secured deletion of the section recognizing "Aboriginal rights," softened only by a promise to take up the Indigenous agenda in a constitutional conference within a year. The vital section — Trudeau's pan-Canadian vision respecting the equality of the French language and the rights of linguistic minorities — remained untouched in the resolution. So, too, did the sections protecting equalization and the new natural resource powers of the provinces.

But when the results of the nocturnal negotiations were released, an incensed Canadian public intervened. Women's groups immediately rose to demand the removal of the notwithstanding clause from their cherished hard-fought equality rights. One by one, they lobbied provincial premiers to rescind this limitation of their rights. That battle was won in a new section 28. Similarly, public demands for rectifying the shameful deletion of Indigenous Rights arose, and, here too, these led to provincial retreats and the restoration of the section. Oddly, there was no similar uprising demanding the removal of the notwithstanding clause over other Charter rights, including fundamental freedoms.

Canada Notwithstanding?[31]

"Notwithstanding" is a tricky word: an essential tool in legal jargon, as in these constitutional documents, it teases that one has a right but then one doesn't. One giveth on the one hand and taketh away on the other. When such an obscure term becomes part of a people's lexicon, when it becomes "entrenched," curiously embedded in the minds and perhaps even subconscious of Canadian citizens, it achieves a unique stature in our culture. What other people in the world could possibly be captured by it?

It's our country's Trojan horse, lurking in section 33 of the Charter, ready to threaten our rights:

> **APPLICATION OF CHARTER**
>
> **32 (1)** This Charter applies
>
> **(a)** to the Parliament and government of Canada … and
>
> **(b)** to the legislature and government of each province.…
>
> […]
>
> **EXCEPTION WHEN EXPRESS DECLARATION**
>
> **33 (1)** Parliament or the legislature of a province may expressly declare in an Act of Parliament or of the legislature, as the case may be, that the Act or a provision thereof shall operate notwithstanding a provision included in section 2 [Fundamental Freedoms] or sections 7 to 15 [Legal and Equality Rights] of this Charter.
>
> […]
>
> **FIVE YEAR LIMITATION**
>
> **(3)** A declaration made under subsection (1) shall cease to have effect five years after it comes into force.…
>
> **RE-ENACTMENT**
>
> **(4)** Parliament or the legislature of a province may re-enact a declaration made under subsection (1).[32]

This clause raised its hoary head at the launch of the Charter. Just as was feared at that time, the override clause has come back to haunt us at several points in our subsequent history, used at once in Quebec as an initial act of protest and several times later, but also recently in New Brunswick (2019), Ontario (2018, 2021), and Saskatchewan (2023). This widespread cavalier disregard of Canadians' constitutional rights and freedoms, often in relatively trivial circumstances, is clearly undermining the Charter. It reached its height when for the first time, a federal leader, Pierre Poilievre, leader of the Conservative Party of Canada, threatened in 2024 to use the clause to override the courts in criminal law cases.

This concession to parliamentary sovereignty was the price paid to get provincial agreement on the Charter. Was it an honourable compromise or "abject failure," as Trudeau flippantly dubbed it? Unquestionably, it is now proving to be a major flaw. Doubtless, ceding to this "mealy-mouthed notwithstanding clause"[33] was deeply regrettable, but it was also a necessity to which Trudeau reluctantly yielded: better a Charter with a notwithstanding clause, he thought, than no Charter at all. Even so, for Charter Canadians, *notwithstanding* is a menace triggered by uttering its very name.

For the Last Time: "Off We Go to Queen and Westminster"

By December 8, 1981, the resolution, complete with all amendments, was passed by the Parliament of Canada and given assent by Canada's Governor General. The following day, it was despatched to Buckingham Palace. The resolution was speedily approved in Great Britain, despite vigorous objections by Quebec's government and by representatives of the Indigenous Peoples. By March 29, it had completed all the necessary stages of legislative approval at Westminster and was signed into law by Queen Elizabeth II. On April 17, 1982, in an outdoor ceremony in Ottawa, the Queen signed and proclaimed the coming into force of the Act, which thereafter marked the end of any British law being applicable to Canada. Patriation — full legal independence — had been finally achieved.

Alberta, as the architect of Canada's new amending formula, celebrated the success it had achieved at the bargaining table. Henceforth, amendments to Canada's Constitution could proceed with the consent of Parliament and seven provinces representing at least fifty per cent of Canada's population. While this formula was well in line with Canada's prior history, it departed sharply from Pierre Trudeau's amendment proposal that would have provided a veto for Quebec and Ontario. In sharp contrast, the official formula now declared the *equality of provinces*. While René Lévesque's government protested strenuously and appealed to the courts for recognition of a veto for Quebec, its claims were wholly rejected. In truth, Quebec's premier had only himself to blame. He had himself gambled unwisely by agreeing to the

Gang of Eight's amendment plan that ceded a veto for Quebec and now was hoisted with his own petard. In a blistering letter in response, Trudeau reminded Lévesque that *he* was the one responsible for the loss of Quebec's veto and that he was unlikely to get it back. Lévesque's humiliation for having bungled at almost every turn was complete.

We Owe the Charter to Him

Canada's "founding fathers" — among them, John A. Macdonald, Canada's first prime minister — may collectively lay claim to fathering our country's first Constitution at Confederation in 1867. Pierre Trudeau joins their illustrious company as the undoubted father of Canada's Charter of Rights and Freedoms, enacted as a new part of our Constitution in 1982. The following are among its protections:

> **FUNDAMENTAL FREEDOMS**
>
> **2** Everyone has the following freedoms:
> **(a)** freedom of conscience and religion;
> **(b)** freedom of thought, belief, opinion and expression, including freedom of the press and other media of communication;
> **(c)** freedom of peaceful assembly; and
> **(d)** freedom of association.[34]

> LEGAL RIGHTS
>
> **LIFE, LIBERTY AND SECURITY OF PERSON**
>
> 7 Everyone has the right to life, liberty and the security of the person....
>
> **SEARCH AND SEIZURE**
>
> **8** Everyone has the right to be secure against unreasonable search or seizure.[35]

EQUALITY RIGHTS

EQUALITY BEFORE AND UNDER LAW AND EQUAL PROTECTION AND BENEFIT OF LAW

> **15 (1)** Every individual is equal before and under the law and has the right to the equal protection and equal benefit of the law without discrimination ... based on race, national or ethnic origin, colour, religion, sex, age or mental or physical disability.[36]

The Charter is Trudeau's honour and his legacy. The reason for this recognition is not that he alone was responsible for it, but that he drove it forward more forcefully than any Canadian leader could or would have done. Never doubting its role in remaking and renewing Canada, he made it central to the federal strategy against Quebec separatism, first as justice minister in Pearson's government and then as prime minister over his many years in office. When he realized that only the threat of unilateral patriation would see it through, and after he had solemnly promised action in Quebec in the 1980 referendum, he went ahead as no other Canadian prime minister would have dared to do.

He knowingly put federalism to its severest test by proceeding unilaterally to amend the Canadian Constitution. Whatever one may think of his critique of the Supreme Court judgment, the Court in effect forced a return to the bargaining table in search of substantial provincial consent for these important additions to Canada's Constitution. It is doubtful that these important amendments, if brought back to Canada unilaterally, would ever have been successful in winning broad, long-term acceptance at home. Not even a national referendum, which Trudeau held out as an ultimate last possibility, would necessarily have brought constitutional peace and legitimacy. In short, he took what he later recognized as the "wiser course" of compromise.

In his *Memoirs*, Trudeau acknowledged that a statesman needs to listen to the wise counsel of his allies (such as Premier Bill Davis) and to know when to accept "second best" with a compromise that's on the table.[37] Despite continuing regrets over concessions respecting both the Charter and the amending formula, he declared: "On the whole, the Constitution Act largely enshrined the values I had been advocating since I wrote my first article in *Cité libre* in 1950."[38] Those values rested on a belief in the sanctity of the individual person with basic inalienable rights that the Charter enshrined "as a system of values such as liberty, equality, and the rights of association that Canadians from coast to coast could share."[39] Even more important was the value he attached to linguistic rights and their role in making Canada a home for both English- and French-speaking Canadians. Trudeau's dream of securing official bilingualism and minority language educational rights throughout the country was now firmly embedded in the Constitution. Here was the pan-Canadian alternative to Quebec separatism. Finally, his values were also affirmed through the dream of patriation, a dream stemming back to Trudeau's days at the Privy Council around 1950, when he watched with irritation Canadians' continuing failure to bring home Canada's Constitution from Britain. He pushed and pushed until that deed was done, ending for good the game of provincial blackmail for its completion. Relentless and consistent with his principles he remained, right to the very end.

While polls showed that these achievements were widely supported by Canadians in every province, there was no disguising the fact that Quebecers felt left out. The majority regretted that Quebec's government and legislature had not signed on to the Charter and that the province had not won any additional powers at all from the constitutional talks. Such was the shameful situation that Quebec nationalists of varying hues felt after Lévesque's negotiating debacle. A hole was left at the centre of Canada-Quebec politics: how could Quebec be brought in? Under what circumstances could the National Assembly of Quebec sign on to Canada's new Constitution? The ground was laid for yet more constitutional talks to come, though Trudeau rather surprisingly seemed to think matters were finally settled in 1982. They were not. The country was not yet done with its addiction to all things constitutional.

SEVEN

The Constitution "Forever and Ever"

Since 1982 the federation was set to last a thousand years! Alas, only one eventuality had not been foreseen: that one day the government of Canada would fall into the hands of a wimp.*

A Brief Reprieve: Patriating the Economy

While the battle over patriation and the Charter of Rights and Freedoms was doubtless the focal point of Trudeau's legacy during his last term in office in the 1980s, there was another initiative launched at about the same time that drew virtually equal fire and fury. Its name was the National Energy Program (NEP), and it was unveiled by Marc Lalonde, minister of energy, on behalf of the Trudeau government on October 28, 1980. On the one hand, this was another policy in the struggle to shore up Ottawa's role against growing provincial power, building up particularly in the rich petroleum provinces in Canada's West. The new program aimed at hiking the share of federal revenue from the energy sector at the expense of the producing provinces and energy companies. Just as important, the policy provided incentives for exploration and development on "Canada Lands" offshore and in the North, to the disadvantage of Western oil-producing provinces.

* Trudeau's withering comment was directed at the then prime minister Brian Mulroney after the Meech Lake Accord was announced. See Donald Johnson, ed., *With a Bang, Not a Whimper: Pierre Trudeau Speaks Out* (Toronto: Stoddart, 1988), 21–22.

On the other hand, the policy responded to growing concerns over foreign ownership in Canada by "patriating the economy" in much the same spirit as it was then pursuing the "patriating of the constitution." The stated policy goal was to "Canadianize" the oil and gas industry by 1990.[1] The rhetoric undergirding this initiative was Canadian patriotism, epitomized by the proud state company, Petro Canada, created in 1975 with Liberal and NDP support, to give Canadians a direct stake both in protecting energy security and in the burgeoning energy economy.

The 1973 worldwide energy crisis — when oil prices quadrupled — was the immediate backdrop to an increasingly nationalist response from countries like Canada, who were seeking to limit the damage to their consumers and manufacturers. Ottawa established a "made in Canada" price for oil, well below the international price, thus undercutting the revenue of domestic and foreign oil producers and of producing provinces. Moreover, oil prices continued to climb over the 1970s, and they were projected to rise even higher in the future. Facing higher costs but declining revenue relative to the oil-producing provinces, Ottawa faced increasingly bleak prospects. The Liberals began to work on the NEP while in opposition as an alternative to the new Joe Clark minority government, which tilted toward a market-driven approach favourable to Western interests and which threatened to privatize Petro Canada.

This Liberal policy of economic nationalism reflected Pierre Trudeau's philosophy of developing the country's economy independently and sharing its wealth fairly. Earlier in the 1970s, he had supported a "Third Option" to the status quo or to growing integration with the U.S. by strengthening the Canadian economy and national life in three specific ways:

- strengthening Canadian ownership of the economy;
- protecting Canadian culture; and
- diversifying Canada's trade abroad.[2]

The Foreign Investment Review Agency, the Canada Development Corporation, and Petro Canada were all earlier instruments of state developed for this purpose. The NEP followed in this tradition, this time to protect the country against soaring energy prices and to strike what Liberals claimed to be a fairer division of revenues between the governments and industry. Trudeau argued the basic fairness of this policy, reminding Westerners that consumers east of the Ottawa river, under the National Oil Policy of the Diefenbaker government, had subsidized the development of the West's energy industry by paying higher than world prices:

> So my argument was that now that prices were going sky-high, the shoe should be on the other foot and we would share in the opposite direction. Alberta would send a greater percentage of its enormous increase in price to the rest of Canada, so that we could afford our equalization payments, and so that we could subsidize those consumers who had to buy overseas oil. That seemed fair enough to me.[3]

To Westerners, this was seen as no less than a frontal assault on their lands and resources, akin to intruders barging in and taking over the "living room." Such shock and trauma would never be forgotten. The NEP became a powerful symbol in the minds of Westerners of Central Canadian domination and Liberal treachery. Foreign multinationals, the American government, and even much of the Canadian business community protested this state intervention and protectionism. However, an agreement was reached in September 1981 between Alberta and Ottawa that saw each side cede some ground in a compromise resolution. Yet the expected rising prices that undergirded the logic of the federal policy went in the opposite direction, falling sharply. So, as Trudeau admitted, "all our planning went for naught," as the money would not be there to support Canadian oil companies and consumers.[4] A few years later, with the election of Brian Mulroney's government in 1984, the political pendulum swung decisively in the opposite direction. With the establishment of a Free Trade Agreement between Canada and the United States in 1988, there was no room for state protectionist policies like the NEP. Petro Canada was later privatized. In short, this part of Trudeau's legacy, unlike his constitutional measures, would not prove enduring.

"The Walk in the Snow" Was No Retirement from the Constitution

If you thought that legendary "walk in the snow" marked Trudeau's final peace and freedom from the "never-ending" Constitution, you'd be dead wrong. The truth is he'd never be free of it. Retirement from the Constitution would not be granted this veteran of Canada's constitutional wars. Nor would his restless soul resist the constant swirl of constitutional politics that engulfed Quebec following the momentous 1982 Constitution Act. In the summer of 1984, he had barely settled into his elegant Art Deco Ernest Cormier House on Pine Avenue in the heart of Montreal than he learned that Lévesque's government had received an invitation to yet another constitutional dance from Canada's new Conservative prime minister, Brian Mulroney. It was to be called the "Quebec Round."

Lévesque had accepted the "beau risque" (worthwhile risk) of engaging with the federal government once again, after two years of "cold shoulder" resistance to the imposition of the 1982 agreement without the consent of Quebec. This odd dalliance between federal Conservatives and the separatist government provoked deep splits within the Parti Québécois, prompting the resignation of René Lévesque and the ultimate defeat of the party in the 1985 election. It would be a Liberal government under veteran premier Robert Bourassa that would then take centre stage for the "Quebec Round," a quiet, even furtive, constitutional dance that would ultimately lead to the 1987 Meech Lake Accord. Pierre Trudeau was astounded that any prime minister would invite back the ghosts of Quebec nationalism and expose the country to the perils that had been so recently defeated.

But bringing Quebec back into the fold of Canada after the rupture of 1982 was simply irresistible politics for Brian Mulroney and he steered the ship of state right onto the shoals of Quebecers' aggrieved nationalism. If this overconfident prime minister could not pull the deed off successfully, the spectre of renewed Quebec separatism would arise again in fury. Mulroney's invitation amounted to a gambler's throw of the dice.

Gil Rémillard, Quebec minister of justice and of intergovernmental affairs, set the terms for a Quebec rapprochement with Ottawa and the other provinces. At Mont-Gabriel on May 9, 1986, he announced five conditions for Quebec to accept the 1982 Constitution Act (though Quebec by law was already fully subject to it):

- the explicit recognition of Quebec as a distinct society;
- a guarantee of increased powers for Quebec in immigration;
- an explicit limitation on the federal spending power;
- recognition of a Quebec right of veto; and
- Quebec's participation in the appointment of judges to the Supreme Court.

Here, once again, Quebec demanded both unique recognition and additional powers if its National Assembly (its provincial legislature here appropriating the name of France's National Assembly) were to sign on to what was already established Canadian constitutional law. This was the price for symbolically re-joining the Canadian constitutional family. In short, talks would focus exclusively on Quebec's nationalist demands, despite the failure of that agenda in the 1980 Quebec referendum and subsequent negotiations.

Indeed, advocates for a Quebec Round argued that Pierre Trudeau had somehow misled Quebecers in the 1980 referendum when he promised renewed federalism, making Quebecers think he was promising recognition of Quebec as a distinct society, or special status. Senator Lowell Murray, a close advisor to Mulroney, argued that such a promise was made and not kept.[5] Prominent Quebec intellectuals like Guy Laforest agreed about the making of the same false promise or at least the allowing for deliberate ambiguity.[6] For Trudeau, such an allegation was absurd. He argued later before the Senate:

> I had been writing, speaking and publishing for some 20 years against any form of special status so how could it reasonably be inferred I was attempting to win the referendum by setting Canada on a course that I consistently denounced as deleterious to the integrity of Canada, as deleterious as even losing the referendum itself would be?[7]

In any event, this was the rupture that the Mulroney government promised to remedy. Yet the process of constitutional politics now unfolded in quite a marked contrast with that of the past. Unlike the prior process, over decades of open public constitutional conferences and private negotiating sessions of officials and first ministers closely monitored by Canadian media, Canadians were confronted with a new secretive, even furtive, style of Mulroney constitution-making. There would be no debate in televised public conferences, nor media coverage, nor even the usual throng of advisers. Instead, Canadians discovered that the Constitution was to be the subject of backroom talks among the "boys" — Canada's eleven first ministers. Huddled together quietly in a retreat on the shores of Meech Lake in the Gatineau Hills, the "boys" hammered out an agreement to amend the Constitution and boldly unveiled the Meech Lake Accord on April 30, 1987. Here was a surprise package that seemed to secure constitutional peace with Quebec. It was initially supported by all governments and even by opposition leaders in the House of Commons. Most Canadians were happy to see the rupture with Quebec resolved, so it looked at first as though Mulroney's backroom throwing of the dice had done the trick.

But the devil, as they say, was in the details. What did it mean to enshrine at the outset of the Canadian Constitution a new clause that the Constitution recognize that "Quebec constitutes within Canada a distinct society" and affirm "the role of the legislature and Government of Quebec to preserve and promote the distinct identity of Quebec?"[8] For premier Bourassa, the answer was clear: "We have for the first time in 120 years of federalism managed to provide constitutional underpinnings for the preservation and promotion of the *French character of Quebec*."[9]

What did it mean to recognize two Canadas as a fundamental characteristic of Canada — a "French-speaking Canada, centered in but not limited to Quebec" and an "English-speaking Canada concentrated outside Quebec but also present in Quebec?" Wasn't this talk of "two Canadas" typical separatist thinking and rhetoric? How could this dualism be reconciled with the entrenchment of a one-Canada bilingual country enacted in 1982 with rights for the linguistic minorities? Good questions indeed! Yet if you looked for a clear answer from the drafters of the Meech Lake Accord, you'd search in vain.

Most leaders in Quebec argued, on the one hand, that "Quebec's specificity" was now a paramount principle in the interpretation of the Constitution and that it would lead to more powers and recognition of its distinct status. On the other hand, federal and provincial leaders outside Quebec argued that it was merely a symbolic principle in recognition of a "sociological reality" and did not confer a special status in law for Quebec. This equivocation among the drafters was not reassuring to the public. It was much the same with the other provisions of the Meech Lake Accord — completely divergent arguments in and outside of Quebec over the meaning and implications of the backroom deal.

Nor was the spectre of backroom deal-making inspiring public confidence. On the contrary, it was engendering public skepticism. The image suggested shady and secretive arrangements among eleven men who were claiming to change the Canadian Constitution over the heads of the people. After making their pact, first ministers declared that there would be changes only in the event of "egregious errors" and pushed for swift enactment by the legislatures that they themselves controlled. Their pact had even ensured everlasting invitations to required annual first ministers' constitutional conferences without end into the future. What would become of the country and its Constitution on this continuous autopilot?

Pierre Trudeau Comes Out Swinging

"It would be better for Canada if the Meech Lake monster went back and drowned itself in the watery depths from which it should never have raised its hideous head."[10] Pierre Trudeau had a way with words, his sarcasm here wrapped in mock gothic horror. He knew how to poke fun in a feisty exchange — in this case, mocking a certain Mr. Adams, a journalist with *Le Devoir*, as "an honest man hiding behind the veil of a hyper nationalist." But the implication in his humour was clear: if the Meech Lake monster wouldn't drown itself, we must — for the sake of Canada — do it. And so that was the task he set for himself on May 27 in a scathing article in *La Presse* and the *Toronto Star*:

> What a magician this Mr. Mulroney is, and what a sly fox!
>
> He has not quite succeeded in achieving sovereignty-association, but he has put Canada on a fast track to getting there ...
>
> What a dark day for Canada was this April 30, 1987! In addition to surrendering to the provinces important parts of its jurisdiction (the spending power, immigration), in addition to weakening the Canadian Charter of Rights, the Canadian state made subordinate to the provinces its legislative power (Senate) and its judicial power (the Supreme Court); and it did this without hope of ever getting it back ...
>
> All this was done under the pretext of "permitting Quebec to fully participate in Canada's constitutional evolution." As if Quebec had not fully participated, right from the beginning, in Canada's constitutional evolution!

Quebec being left out was an excuse that Trudeau dismissed as fiction. He put the blame for Meech Lake on politicians seeking "political advantages." How happy were all provincial premiers to downplay the duty of promoting one-Canada bilingualism in favour of two linguistic Canadas,

> where Quebec will be French, Canada will be English, and we will all be friends. This is what Mr. Lévesque used to be preaching [Trudeau told the Senate]; you speak English in your provinces and we will speak French in ours ... I say that is really welching on a deal [agreed to in the Constitution Act, 1982, where language rights for minorities would be protected in the whole of Canada.][11]

Similarly, those premiers who had always fought against the Charter of Rights now could weaken its protection of individual rights in favour of "collective rights" in the linguistic enclave of a "distinct society." Trudeau argued that this would invariably lead to a hierarchy of rights in Quebec, where individuals who were not "pure laine" Québécois — Indigenous Peoples, immigrants, the English-speaking minority — would find their rights compromised in favour of a linguistic majoritarian nationalism.

And what did he make of the widespread claim that the distinct society clause was recognizing Quebec as the "homeland of the French-speaking people of Canada"? This framing, he felt, would lead to dubious linguistic bifurcation of the country. Because the Meech Accord seemed to enshrine such an idea, many wondered whether it was true. Doubtless, Quebec had the highest number of French-speaking people in Canada and was the only province with a French-speaking majority, but would this make it a "homeland" for *all* French-speaking people, especially those living outside Quebec? How would Acadians, as a distinct francophone people with a long history of their own living throughout Atlantic Canada, feel to be so framed and designated? Or the Métis people in Manitoba, or, in fact, the million-strong French-speaking minority in Ontario? These communities all recognized and supported Trudeau's policy of bilingualism and the Charter as their shield and Canada as their homeland. In truth, it seemed odd, if not pretentious, for Quebec to paint itself as the homeland of the French-speaking people of Canada. Yet such were the rhetorical sweep and implications of the Meech Lake Accord.

Trudeau warned of the dangers of privileging provincial patriotism over truly national Canadian patriotism. He invoked the memory of the great Henri Bourassa and praised his dream of a pan-Canadian nationalism encompassing French and English rights, which would be stronger than any provincial patriotism, including Quebec's.[12] Such was the Trudeau vision that animated his time in office and sustained his opposition later as a private citizen to the constitutional handiwork of his successors.

Alas, the Meech Lake "monster" did not die by quietly drowning itself. It expired when its makers could not garner the unanimous consent needed to give it "breath of life," despite three long years of effort from 1987 to 1990. In the course of that time, three of the Meech signatories had been replaced by new premiers who had campaigned against it and were no longer bound to it. Yet the Meech Lake Accord still received the assent of the Parliament and of eight provincial legislatures representing 96 percent of the population.

Certainly, this showed that, contrary to Québécois nationalist arguments, English-speaking Canada had not rejected the Meech Lake Accord.

Yet Quebecers were fully aware of the rising tide of public opinion in English-speaking Canada opposed to the Accord. This had reached a crescendo after the Bourassa government in 1988 used the notwithstanding clause to overturn the Supreme Court's decision striking down Bill 178, which prohibited any language but French on signs in Quebec. The premier declared that if the Meech Lake Accord were in place, he would not have had to use the notwithstanding clause. This caused Premier Filmon in Manitoba to halt consideration of the Accord for a long time. While the Manitoba legislature finally appeared ready to approve it near the final deadline and repeatedly tried to bring the matter to a vote by moving a motion for emergency debate requiring members' unanimous consent, Indigenous leader Elijah Harper stood in the way, refusing his consent *eight* times between June 12 and June 21. Proudly holding an eagle feather in solemn opposition, with National Chief Phil Fontaine and fellow Chiefs looking on jubilantly from the legislative gallery, he ran out the clock, preventing Manitoba's required legislative approval. This decision rendered the matter of further ratification redundant and gave Premier Clyde Wells the grounds for cancelling the vote on the Accord in the provincial legislature of Newfoundland and Labrador. The Meech Lake monster was thus removed from its "life support." So ended this failed experiment with recognizing duality and Quebec's distinctiveness in the Canadian Constitution.

There was huge disappointment over the end of this dream of dualism, especially among authors like Guy Laforest, who saw in it the denial of André Laurendeau's gentle vision.[13] But among hard nationalists, who had always dismissed the Meech Lake Accord's weak embroidering of sovereignty, there was only cold fury at what they claimed, quite falsely, was a total rebuff from English-speaking Canada.

Trudeau, once again donning the role of the polemicist, had defeated the advocates of special status for Quebec, just as he had earlier, as prime minister in the negotiations of 1982, outfoxed Lévesque and PQ sovereigntist hardliners. Brian Mulroney was dismissed as a "weakling" and his dice-rolling at Meech Lake a dismal failure. The constitutional rupture between

Quebec and the rest of Canada in June 1990, set in play a second time by Pierre Trudeau, was complete — a national unity crisis more serious than at any other time in Canadian history. In this collision, Trudeau thought, if Canada were to go, better that it be with a "bang than a whimper."[14]

Such decisiveness in the face of a crisis was wholly typical of Trudeau's statesmanship — whether defiantly facing projectiles in a showdown with a 1968 Jean Baptiste rally or rejecting kidnapping and death threats in October 1970 or daring to go it alone to achieve patriation and a Charter of Rights — he was always ready to take big but calculated risks to preserve and promote Canada. In this, as we shall argue in our concluding overview, Trudeau was an extraordinary master of daring realist statecraft.

Lurching from the "Quebec Round" to the "Canada Round"

Blinded and stumbling, such was Canada post-Meech. In Quebec and elsewhere, there was a flurry of commissions and consultations. The Allaire Report, basking in hyper-nationalist Québécois opinion after the defeat of Meech Lake, demanded a wholesale transfer of federal powers to Quebec. Sovereigntists looked forward to a second referendum on Quebec independence, now promised by Premier Robert Bourassa "to keep a knife at the throat of English-Canada." The Mulroney government launched a variety of consultation exercises — the Spicer Commission to allow venting on all sides, a veritable "bitch fest," then an ill-fated Beaudoin-Dobbie Parliamentary Committee that ran aground mid-way through its mandate. The process was only retrieved by Ottawa then empowering public policy institutes to hold televised "Renewal of Canada Conferences" in the winter of 1992 to review its constitutional proposals in the document *Shaping Canada's Future Together*, unveiled in September 1991.[15]

This was the beginning of what became known as the "Canada Round," which openly invited wide public participation in debate and discussion of proposals. In marked contrast to the secretive "First Ministers Only" negotiations of Meech Lake,[16] Ottawa had learned its lesson and, under the new constitution minister, Joe Clark, reversed course and adopted the most open-ended process of constitutional politics Canada had ever seen. With the televised Renewal of Canada Conferences, hundreds of participants joined in broad public debate of the federal constitutional proposals, ultimately submitting these to their fate in conference outcomes. In their concluding sessions, these conferences decided to accept or reject the actual proposals of the federal government. Joe Clark also invited in Indigenous leaders as participants in the debates over Indigenous self-government and for the first time gave them a seat at the negotiating table alongside first ministers. Later, as these multilateral discussions proceeded over several months, an announcement was made in August 1992 of an agreement known as the Charlottetown Accord.

Once again, Mulroney was throwing the dice, this time seeking an all-or-nothing, wholesale resolution of all of Canada's constitutional grievances. Outsiders were scratching their heads, wondering what was going on in Canada that this fine country should find itself in apparent everlasting turmoil? Canada seemed to be suffering from an addiction to "constitutionalitis." The country just couldn't or wouldn't leave it alone.

Nor, of course, could Pierre Elliott Trudeau. It wasn't long before he emerged from his lair. On October 1, 1992, he was the featured speaker at the venerable *Cité libre* lecture at the Maison Egg Roll, a Chinese restaurant in St. Henri, Montreal. The country held its breath, awaiting his pronouncement on the new Accord, which was then being submitted for approval to the people of Canada in a national referendum. How would Pierre Trudeau not relish the opportunity, on this dear familiar platform, to pronounce his verdict. Predictably, he dismissed the Charlottetown Accord, the work of "doddering fools," as "a mess that deserves a big NO."[17]

The polemicist was back. He had lost none of his biting invective, honed over his *Cité libre* years as a journalist. His arguments were like those he had brandished against the Meech Lake monster, although this time they were lawyerly: he parsed and pulled apart the many elements in the new "Canada Clause":

> Oh I see, they want to please everybody. You, over here, you say you are committed to a society where collective rights are tops? OK. In your neck of the woods, people are "committed" to collective rights. And you, over there, you

> prefer that individual rights win out? That's quite all right, we are committed to your individual rights too. But what happens when a contradiction arises?
>
> [Worse still] we haven't seen the actual text. All we've seen is this *thing* [the Consensus Report] where citizens will have to be satisfied with generalities.... They tell us don't worry about it, nobody will have to choose between collective rights and individual rights, since *both* are recognized. Well, really!

Trudeau asked his audience why Canada was again thrown into constitutional disarray, starting right over again — with scarcely a breather — after the defeat of Meech Lake:

> He [Mr. Mulroney] failed with Meech Lake, so why did he try all over again when it wasn't working? He started again *because he saw he was going to lose his friend Lucien Bouchard if he didn't start up again*, and he would lose others unless he offered a distinct society to Quebec nationalists.[18]

Canada, under these circumstances, faced interminable demands upon compliant, obliging politicians and the Constitution could not be put to rest for any reasonable length of time. Trudeau reminded his audience that that was exactly what Mr. Bourassa and Mr. Rémillard were promising for the future.

> You think you will have peace and quiet if you vote YES! You will have peace and quiet if you vote NO, because NO means we are fed up with the Constitutional debate, and we don't want to hear about it any more.[19]

Perhaps Canadians weighed this sage advice when they voted down the Charlottetown Accord on referendum night, October 26, 1992. It had been a fractious debate across the country, with opposition animated by disparate issues in different parts of the country but with substantial levels of moderate support and compromise too. The popular vote was 54 percent NO and 46 percent YES. The Atlantic provinces, the Northwest Territories, and Ontario voted YES, while all the Western provinces voted decisively NO, as did Quebec itself. The latter provinces were always the most constitutionally restless in the country. If there was a silver lining in the referendum outcome, it was that a majority in *both* English Canada and Quebec voted thumbs-down on the Charlottetown Accord.

Yet the defeat should not be exaggerated. The division in the overall national vote was not so great, suggesting remarkable patience in the country after three decades of constitutional politics. Nor was Canada unusual in rejecting in a national referendum change to the country's Constitution. Comparative international experience has often shown strong public reluctance to endorse constitutional changes by referendum. The odds of success in Canada were almost insuperable, since our amendment procedures required in this case a positive vote in *every* province of Canada. No such hurdle had ever been required before. Yet Mulroney's government pressed ahead anyway.

The Reckoning: Quebec Votes on Sovereignty a Second Time in 1995

For constitutional bunglers, there shall be a reckoning. Quebec had solemnly warned that failure would lead to a second secessionist referendum. With Premier Jacques Parizeau in charge of a new hardline PQ government elected in 1994, Quebec independence would be on the ballot within a year. Brian Mulroney was no longer around to face the music, since the Conservative Party had been virtually wiped out in the 1993 election. It was Jean Chrétien and the federal Liberals in power in Ottawa, and Daniel Johnson Jr., Liberal leader of the NO campaign in Quebec, who were left to defend Canada after dashed hopes and constitutional ruin. Never had the spectre of Quebec separatism loomed so large.

This was particularly the case when charismatic federal Bloc Québécois leader, Lucien Bouchard, joined the YES campaign alongside Premier

Parizeau. Polls then began to show a rise in separatist sentiment indicating a possible majority YES vote. The tightening of the vote in the campaign brought in Prime Minister Chrétien with promises of parliamentary recognition of Quebec as a "distinct society" and of an indirect Quebec veto, presumably to be honoured by all future parliaments. These frail political declarations, of course, were not quite the same thing as putting these protections into the constitutional law of Canada. At the last stages, a large federal "unity rally" in Montreal was held to boost federalist forces. The referendum question again made the offer of economic association with the rest of Canada a part of the sovereignty vote. Yet Premier Parizeau had determined that he would in any event make a unilateral declaration of independence in the event of a YES victory.

But where was Pierre Trudeau at this crucial time? From him, there was only silence. He was not officially invited to speak on behalf of the NO vote; nor did he choose to intervene, as he had before with the Meech Lake and Charlottetown Accords. Respecting the referendum managers, he sat it out. On this occasion, the debate and vote went ahead without him.

The results were a shocking cliff-hanger: this time, the NO vote ticked in at a bare 50.58 percent of the vote, while the YES vote stood at 49.42 percent. This was an agonizing outcome for both Canada and for Quebec. Barely a sliver of comfort for Canadian unity, it was a crushing blow for nationalists in a sovereignty referendum boasting 93.5 percent participation. Jacques Parizeau, announcing his resignation as premier, bitterly denounced the results, blaming them on the marked opposition of "ethnics and money" compared to a 60 plus percent YES vote among francophones. The scars and division amongst Quebecers, in such an emotionally wrenching fundamental decision, would take a long time to heal.

Though there was idle talk of opening constitutional talks again, there was no longer any appetite for it. Ontario flatly refused to consider the idea. The Constitution would finally be put on ice for the foreseeable future. Quebecers had no stomach for more division and dissension, and English-speaking Canadians were thoroughly sick of all things constitutional. Thirty years of constitutional wrangling was finally coming to a close. But the scare of this second Quebec referendum was not forgotten. There was growing awareness that Canada had come very close to severe crisis without once clarifying the country's basic legal rules and understandings around secessionist referendums. Stéphane Dion, the new minister of intergovernmental affairs in Chrétien's cabinet, sought from the Supreme Court of Canada clear answers to the following Reference questions:

- Under the Constitution of Canada, can the National Assembly, legislature, or government of Quebec effect the secession of Quebec from Canada unilaterally?
- Does international law give the National Assembly, legislature, or government of Quebec the right to effect the secession of Quebec from Canada unilaterally?

The Supreme Court in 1998 gave a definitive NO answer to both these questions. It also indicated that the government of Canada would have an obligation to negotiate if a clear majority of Quebecers voted for secession in response to a clear question. Such negotiations would take place within the framework of the existing Canadian Constitution and amendment procedures, and any settlement would have to respect the principle of democracy, including the rights of individuals and minorities. After publicly sparring with Premier Lucien Bouchard, in December 1999, Minister Dion introduced into the House of Commons the Clarity Act, which stipulated that separation negotiations would take place only if the House of Commons had previously accepted that the referendum question was properly framed to voters in terms of independence and that the result would have to be a "clear majority" in favour rather than a "50 percent plus one" majority. The Clarity Act became law in March 2000.

Though well grounded in the decision of the Supreme Court, the Clarity Act was boldly rejected by Quebec's National Assembly just two days after its introduction in the House of Commons. The PQ government introduced its own Bill 99, claiming the right of the Quebec people and the Quebec State to determine the sovereignty question and majority on its own terms. This amounted to little more than political posturing in defiance of the law set down by the Supreme Court. Parizeau-like "unilateral declarations of independence" in future will clearly be recognized as unlawful. Secessionist politics will presumably now operate under clearer rules than they had in the whole "Wild West" phase of Quebec question-setting and unilateral action. Yet it remains to be seen whether sovereigntist politics can be contained by such legalistic framing.

In our view, the Supreme Court judgment in the Quebec Secession Reference dealt in fair and reasonable terms with the question and provided Canada with mature and liberal guidelines. We would be well advised to respect this judgment in future and even to recommend its reasoning to other countries that have scarcely begun to walk very far along this secessionist road. Compare Canada, for example, to the choices of other democratic countries with secession referendums. Spain has ruled out the option altogether and has jailed separatist leaders for daring even to put such a question to its "nation" of Catalonia within the Spanish state. Take the nation of Scotland in the United Kingdom, where its highest court has declared that Scotland cannot have a referendum on secession without the permission of the Parliament at Westminster. In contrast, Canada has twice accepted and participated in Quebec referendums, even with unclear, dubious questions. No longer, perhaps, will the game of secession be played in a fast and loose manner. Clarity is surely a boon for democracy, whatever the outcome of the vote on independence.

EIGHT

Conclusion

PIERRE ELLIOTT TRUDEAU DIED IN HIS MONTREAL HOME ON SEPTEMBER 28, 2000. Eighty years of life. That's what he was given. We have traced his "life of the mind" — his intellectual biography — in two earlier volumes, first as a youth imbued with fierce Québécois nationalism and unbending Catholic faith, and then we have followed him as he acquired a vast and broader intellectual depth of mind at Harvard, Sciences Po, and LSE. That paradoxical foundation of *faith* and intellectual *thought* shaped Pierre Trudeau thereafter as both a liberal "man of the world" and a Christian social democrat committed to a just society. Hence, his deep respect, derived from the study of American and British protection of individual rights, merged with his attachment to Nicolas Berdyaev's personalism — its idyll of liberty and shared brotherly patriotism. For Trudeau, this respect for individual freedom within communal life was the natural foundation of a Just Society.

But this brotherly patriotism should never be confused with the frequently virulent modern nationalisms that depend on building an intolerant "we" against outsiders. We now better understand this exclusionary primordial psychology built into the very nature of human beings. It is a fundamental challenge to just politics in all diverse multicultural societies, as Yascha Mounk's *The Great Experiment* has argued.[1] Pierre Trudeau noted this pathogenic feature in his studies of nationalism, saw its corrosive effects in many countries during his extensive international travels, and lamented its ugly rise to an absolute height in the 1960s in his homeland of Quebec. He understood how shouts like "France for the French," "Quebec for Quebecers," or "Let's Stop the Muslim Flood" work as powerful divisive slogans. In this way, groups turn into entities that define themselves, not in terms of love of others, but in terms of repudiating the "Other." Such nationalism is a "terrible sin against the image of God in man,"[2] inherently unjust, and politically poisonous. These sentiments, drawn from a lifetime regimen of faith, study, and travel at the advent of the postwar age, formed the heart of Trudeau's thinking and ultimately became a bedrock of conviction for the statesman he sought to be and would become.

We called him a "Son of Quebec." So he was, and so he remained. Trudeau was a Montrealer *par excellence*, with deep family roots — francophone *and* anglophone ancestry — stretching back into Quebec's rural past. He never lost sight of that family history nor of his identity as a Quebecer concerned with the fate of his homeland. The Jesuit education he received at Jean-de-Brébeuf instilled in him a duty as a member of the next generation's elite to know and protect the small French-speaking community of Quebec as it stood virtually besieged in a vast English-speaking North America. That was the dilemma for the post-Duplessis elite:, how could Quebec in all its distinctiveness best *survive* and *modernize* in such a context? No one thought longer and harder on that question than Pierre Trudeau, and his thinking and politics evolved constantly. At one time or another, he espoused both separatism and federalism, collective rights and individual rights, and even fascism pre-WWII and liberalism afterward. His mind covered the whole gambit as he emerged from Quebec in the 1920s and 1930s and encountered the wider world of post-war thought. He came to intellectual maturity by the time he was thirty, after which he returned to Quebec with a liberal cast of mind to join the fight for the modernization of his Quebec homeland and for a better, more just, and more tolerant country of Canada.

There was bound to be a struggle with a resistant Quebec past. So, how did Trudeau arm himself for that battle? He did so

- as a lawyer, especially of constitutional law;
- as an intellectual, especially of federalism and human rights; and
- as a journalist, delighting in the sheer invective power of the pen.

He would write and speak in all these roles with uncommon power and brilliance against those whom he saw as enemies in Quebec and in Canada. He would join with like-minded friends in founding a journal of progressive thought, *Cité libre*, to fight authoritarianism and narrow-minded nationalism. Ultimately, this intellectual warrior knew that one day he must be prepared to be a politician, in earnest pursuit of the lofty status of statesman. As we have seen, he asserted in his application to Harvard University that this was to be his life career and ambition, and that he hoped to be worthy of the task.

In due course, this project became not just an intellectually driven life history for Pierre Trudeau, but, by sheer political fortune, a country's destiny. In an oddly fateful way, we can look at this political actor and his "country/homeland" of Canada/Quebec as a case study in applied intellectual biography and not least in the whims of fortune. How likely, after all, would a young man's intellectual dreams and aspirations turn out to come true? That this son of Quebec, Pierre Elliott Trudeau, could implement his vision, and make himself a father of Canada? Yet it came to be. Now in the shadow of his ideas and statesmanship, what do we make of it? The debate over the Trudeau legacy is, even now, sharp and lively, almost as vigorous as when he lived and fought among us.

Was Trudeau's a Case of "Misconceiving Canada"?

This is the book title and bold charge of political scientist Kenneth McRoberts.[3] It is not unlike other similar critiques that seek to show that Trudeau's constitutional plan for a bilingual Canada under a rights Charter has failed the test of national unity. This claim is advanced despite evidence that national unity concerns have receded considerably in the last three decades, that the Charter of Rights and Freedoms has been embraced by Canadians in all parts of the country, and that separatism appears to have plateaued in Quebec. McRoberts no sooner acknowledges this evidence of success for Trudeau's one-Canada civic nationalism than he brushes it aside in favour of a multi-ethnic structuring of Canada. The country for him comprises several nations, and he privileges these communities of "deep diversity"[4] over a one-Canada of universal individual rights. But it is not obvious how a restructuring of Canada along multiple national lines — an archipelago of English, French, and Indigenous nations — would even work, much less improve Canada. McRoberts criticizes Trudeau for refusing to accept ethnic nationalism in Quebec and elsewhere. It's unlikely that Trudeau would be impressed by such an argument nor by a plea that he abdicate his whole life's vision as statesman.

Of course, Trudeau was accustomed to criticism. Indeed, rarely has a person in politics suffered more vitriol from his homeland in life and in death. To speak out as he did against his own countrymen — especially against the nationalist tide that swept so many friends and associates in Quebec — was no small thing. To criticize the narrow-mindedness of English-speaking Canadians in their resistance to a fundamental reform of Confederation also made him few friends on that side of the two solitudes. Clearly, Trudeau had not set out to be an easy, obliging politician but rather an iconoclast, pushing Canadians out of their group complacencies and prejudices. And for that, he paid a price.

And could the constitutional remaking of Canada really have been done without knocking heads? Without adopting the ways of a sly fox at one moment and of an audacious lion at another? He hadn't opted for timid politics during easy political times but for boldness in challenging, dangerous times. His goal was nothing less than to save his homeland and country from self-induced destruction. As he quipped in the 1968 election, he was in politics to prevent a delusional Quebec from walking out of Canada and an exasperated English-speaking Canada from throwing Quebec out in sheer narrow-mindedness. In short, a winning strategy would employ reason over passion and would counter emotional exclusionary "groupism" with liberal reform.[5]

Similarly, he argued that there must be limits to the claims of every ethnic nation to be a state, a halt to endless assertions of a "natural" right to self-determination and sovereignty. Such an intoxicating doctrine, he noted, would swiftly lead to the widespread state dismemberment of multinational countries and international disorder. On the contrary, Trudeau thought that liberal democratic states like Canada, with a federal system of government and a strong Charter of Rights and Freedoms, could function well without tearing themselves apart into ethnic national fragments. His stern advice: beware of drinking too deeply at the well of nationalism.

This is wise advice. Quebec intellectuals, like Guy Laforest and others, have recognized the "totalizing" nature of Quebec nationalism during its heyday from the 1960s to the 1990s.They have also recognized the complicated nature and appeal of Canada in the minds of Quebecers.[6] Moreover, a "two Canada" vision of ethnic French- and English-Canadian nations — two solitudes — is a simplistic illusion given the real multicultural nature of Canada today.[7] Moreover, we are modern and mature people, having taken on a host of complex identities and attachments. We need to remember how far we have changed before we plunge once again into reductionist, separatist politics. The PQ party, headed by the young Paul St-Pierre Plamondon, is leading in the polls as we write and has promised, if elected, to put forward a third Quebec referendum before the year 2030. That is, after all, the reason for the party's existence. Over the course of time, with elections and rotations in office, separatist parties may have opportunities to return to power, and when they do, the question of separatism will certainly arise, so long as that idea commands the attraction of a wide segment of society. The dream of Quebec independence has therefore not gone away and indeed may never do so. But it is likely to face stronger headwinds than in the past.

This battle of dreams forms the heart of this book. PQ leaders and Pierre Trudeau — invoking completely different visions of Quebec/Canada — fought it out from the 1960s to the 1990s, and ethnic nationalists lost every time: two referendums, the constitutional battle over patriation and the Charter of Rights and Freedoms, the Meech Lake Accord, then Charlottetown. For Trudeau, there could be no compromise with secession nor with the cynical politics of ethnic nationalism, famously parodied by Jacques Parizeau as the game of "plucking the chicken."

"Plucking the Chicken": A Slow Death for Canada in Quebec

Jacques Parizeau crafted this apt and colourful metaphor to explain sovereigntist thinking and strategy in a paper he gave in 1968 in France to an international symposium on Canada. He boldly declared:

> To set the problem of separatism forthrightly, it is clear that a majority of Quebecers are against it. Yet, the continuous recuperation of powers [from Ottawa to Quebec] in one area after another is invariably a winning political strategy, even though it is evident that by plucking the chicken one feather at a time eventually it will perish.[8]

Parizeau chuckled as he went on to explain to his audience how PQ leaders used nationalism and that the "threat of rejection [secession] from the existing political order by one of the two ethnic [founding] groups is such a convenient bargaining tool that it inevitably becomes a temptation of every moment."[9] This strategy then attracts the support of other premiers eager to "gang up" and ride on Quebec's demands for more powers. Such was the nationalist strategy of weakening the federal government in the Canadian federation while awaiting the right moment for a vote on outright independence.

This game was scarcely news to Trudeau, who had denounced the resort to nationalism during the Quiet Revolution as "too cheap for the politicians to neglect." He called the sovereigntist project a "massive hoax" perpetrated on the Canadian people. As justice minister, he resisted the Pearson government's growing tendency to be played as a "plucked chicken" as Quebec politicians "opted out" of national federal programs in their territory. Hence, Quebec's post-Duplessis elites sketched out two starkly different strategies for positioning a modern Quebec in the Northern American context. The sovereigntist strategy saw an independent francophone state of Quebec, fortified by a strong internal sense of nationalism, as the best foundation for future success. Such a state would preserve mutually profitable economic links with English Canada within a broad North American trade framework. While there was a time in Trudeau's youth when he too would have championed such a strategy, he later reasoned that Quebec's best interests would be better served within a renewed bilingual federal Canada that provided shelter to its small French-speaking populations. Not only would such a strategy be attractive "as a system worth defending on its own merits, but also as a kind of geo-political buffer ideally suited to the protection of the French fact in the North American context."[10] Using a rights Charter to bind together the citizenry of Canada against the sirens' call of ethnic nationalisms, and ensuring national language rights for the two major linguistic founding peoples, this ambitious plan would best protect *both* Quebec and Canada. It would fulfill the promise of partnership between the French and the English-speaking peoples that, for great French-Canadian leaders like Henri Bourassa, lay at the heart of Confederation.[11]

McRoberts wants to deny that Trudeau's vision had any roots in Quebec's intellectual history.[12] This is untrue. Trudeau himself, in his attack on the Meech Lake Accord, openly paid tribute to Henri Bourassa's idea of a powerful bilingual Canadian nationalism respecting the equality of the races and protective of minority religious and language communities in the provinces. Long before Quebec's Quiet Revolution, this was the spirit of partnership that was embedded in French-Canadian ideas of Confederation. This partnership operated alongside the dream of autonomy that federalism promised Quebec and the other provinces. Confederation was in this sense a bargain in good faith at both levels of the federation: autonomy at home, and shared partnership in the new nation of Canada.

Canada Passing Through a "National Crisis"

We have seen that when Trudeau entered politics, he had little interest in plunging into constitutional politics, dismissing it as a "can of worms." Yet neither he nor the Pearson government could avoid the subject after Ontario's premier John Robarts, in response to Quebec's Quiet Revolution, had called an unprecedented constitutional conference in 1967 to address these concerns. The Bilingual and Bicultural Commission (B&B) had already declared that Canada was passing through a national crisis that required confronting the status of the two "founding peoples." Its recommendation to make Canada an officially bilingual country had led to the

Official Languages Act in 1969 as a step toward accommodating the aspirations of French-speaking Canadians.[13] Carrying out that inclusive vision now became a federal priority. Trudeau accepted this route toward national reconciliation and later sought to take it forward much more decisively by incorporating it into the Constitution of Canada as part of a Charter of Rights and Freedoms.

However, Trudeau's bilingual policy did not depend on constitutional politics alone. He began to set in place policies to change the face of the federal cabinet and the bureaucracy in Ottawa. For example, in the past, francophones had held few if any important positions in cabinet. With Trudeau in power, there were more francophones than anglophones in his cabinet. French was put on a more equal footing in government institutions. The capital itself became more truly bilingual. After the enactment of Trudeau's policies, it became unthinkable for a future prime minister *not* to be bilingual, nor would unilingual federal ministers be long tolerated. This was a sea change from the Ottawa that Trudeau confronted as a francophone working in the Ottawa civil service in the late 1940s. Ottawa now offered career opportunities for fluent bilingual Quebecers to come and work for Canada, just as it encouraged greater respect for the status of the French language, as shown by the growth of early French immersion schooling throughout English Canada. Indeed, McRoberts, while noting the rapid assimilation of francophones outside Canada's bilingual belt, acknowledges that in many respects Trudeau's bilingualism strategy was successful in winning over much of English Canada to this new national policy.

In Quebec, however, where defensive nationalist and separatist thinking remained the elite's default option, there was a frontal attack on bilingualism and, instead, a reliance upon a French-only official language policy. Robert Bourassa's Bill 22 in 1974 and its successor PQ Bill 101 three years later set the pace for official unilingualism in Quebec. This guaranteed ongoing bitter fights over language rights between the francophone majority and linguistic minorities. While there remained constitutional protection in certain areas for the English-language minority in the Constitution Act, 1967, the Canada Act, 1982, and the Official Languages Act, Quebec did not hesitate to use the notwithstanding clause to override Supreme Court decisions declaring that the complete elimination of alternative languages on public signs in the province was unlawful, excessive, and discriminatory.

Bill 96, passed under Francois Legault's government in 2022, extended restrictions against languages other than French in municipalities and in the health and business sectors. The insertion of the notwithstanding clause pre-emptively — at the very outset of the legislative process in this case — was a blatant attempt by Quebec legislators to shield legislation from future court review. Hence, the fight for individual and minority rights against linguistic majoritarian nationalism remains no less a hot "political potato" today than in Pierre Trudeau's day. Similarly, Trudeau's trenchant critique of Quebec nationalism remains no less relevant.

Ironically, Pierre Trudeau's dream has had its least traction in his own home province. This is wholly understandable given the insecurity that a small French-speaking community naturally feels in an English-speaking North American continent. Such is the delicate psychological situation in which Quebecers find themselves. And so, this is the ground upon which nationalists and separatists play, stirring up fears and insecurities over the French language in Quebec to suit their political agenda.[14] Since language is at the heart of Quebec's national identity, it is natural that Quebecers would be susceptible to fears for or threats to language and would give language primacy in any conflict over minority rights. In short, the success of bilingualism depends on Quebecers' own confidence in the strength and predominance of the French language without the need for highly restrictive measures. So far that confidence appears to be lacking.

However, federalism has proven that the province can accommodate the fierce politics around language issues without recourse to Quebec independence and exit from the Canadian union. Quebec government policy in enforcing the French language and francophone economic success in countering former English predominance in business have had the effect of reassuring Quebecers that a federal system of government can work to preserve their unique collective identity. Separatism has declined sharply in Quebec, leaving parties like the PQ with the dilemma of downplaying and then restoring a sovereignty referendum option in the recent party's platform. In effect, the party is caught between a mainstay of separatist supporters and a new generation of Quebecers who, unlike the core nationalist cohort of the 1960s and 1970s, do not see sovereignty as a logical next step in Quebec's modernization.

Federalism Works: It Was Always a Better Solution

So, federalism has prevailed against two generations of nationalist and separatist turmoil in Canada. The country has endured decades of doubt. Progress has been made, chiefly in expanding the rights and freedoms of all Canadians, in guaranteeing equality of opportunity amongst regions, and in strengthening official minority-language communities and various other classes of citizens. The federation has been liberalized far beyond its Confederation framing, but the basic constitutional architecture of Canada has otherwise stood firm. Reinforcing the Charter of Rights and Freedoms, federalism enshrines freedom and substantial autonomy for provinces of deep diversity while retaining the country's freedom and power to act as a rich, prosperous nation in the world. Such is Canada's blessing:

- Unity in diversity.
- Shared sovereignty.

Federal systems are smart and sophisticated. They comprise the most advanced political systems of government in the world today. The spirit of federalism implies tolerance, acknowledgement, and provision for differences amongst diverse communities, providing self rule AND shared rule simultaneously. Federalism is a popular and practical idea that is widely adopted because it fits the actual circumstances of many large, diverse, multicultural societies today. It enshrines multi-level governance *within* a country and, as circumstances require, *above* the state too, in transnational structures like the European Union, continental trade agreements, and the like. These polities are not built to celebrate inward politics and tribal allegiances but are outward-looking, fostering broader co-operative and competitive purposes. As Trudeau deepened his understanding of federalism after years of intense study and life abroad, it became an article of faith and philosophy that he brought back to Canada. He knew and cared little for federalism in his youth but affirmed it unreservedly as an elder statesman.

Yet, as we've shown, the drift away from Canada was well underway in Quebec by the early 1960s. Quebecers increasingly turned inward toward the provincial sphere and toyed with the idea of the separation of Quebec from the rest of Canada. As Trudeau put it:

> The Quebec political classes were bent on emphasizing the defence of French Quebec rather than the advancement of *all* Quebeckers and of francophones of other provinces. Hence, Quebec politicians were infatuated with turns of phrases that implied a loosening of federal principles: "Special Status," "Distinct Society," "Equality or Independence," "Sovereignty-Association."[15]

Though a strong advocate of provincial autonomy, Trudeau argued that in any fundamental conflict of identities, the national will must prevail. There could be no room in a federal country for pitting provincial against national identity or of choosing, for example, Quebec nationalism over Canadian. Why inflict upon each person in that province the perennial question: "Are you a Quebecer or a Canadian?" In a federal system, of course, you are *both*. Trudeau wrote:

> The feeling of being a Canadian, that individual feeling which we must cultivate, the feeling of being loyal to something which is bigger than the province or the city in which we happen to live, must be based on a protection of the basic rights of the citizen, of an access by that citizen to a fair share of the abundance of wealth in this country and to the richness and diversity of its laws. In that sense, the national interest must prevail over the regional interest, difficult as it is for some of us sometimes to set aside our feelings as citizens of this town or inhabitants of that province, because the provincial governments and other groups are there to speak of their interests. That is their duty and that is what they are elected for. But we are elected to speak

> for all of Canada, and if a person cannot feel that in any part of the country he or she will get a fair share, then they will transfer their loyalty from the whole to the particular part of the country in which they choose to live.... That concept of sharing can only be guaranteed, I repeat, if there is a national government which is prepared to state that the national interest must prevail in any situation of conflict over regional differences.[16]

For more than a generation during the height of Quebec nationalism, Trudeau defended federalism, blocked Quebec separatism and special status, and took giant steps toward a more free, tolerant, and just Canada. Father of the Charter of Rights and Freedoms, he laid down his firm legacy as statesman. Trudeau died at the beginning of this century, but his dream lives on. After all, at this stage in our country's maturity, who would dare bet against "rights and freedoms" for the people of Canada?

Acknowledgements

WE WANT TO THANK DEAR FRIENDS AND COLLEAGUES AT SENIOR COLLEGE, UNIVERSITY of Toronto, for their constant support and encouragement of our work. In that regard, we are especially grateful for two research grants from the Research Committee of Senior College to assist in bringing *Trudeau as Statesman* to completion.

We want to recognize Merrijoy Kelner, together with Daphne and Charlie Maurer, who kindly agreed to read and comment on early drafts of chapters. We owe a great deal to the late Peter Russell, noted constitutional expert, who took an exceptional interest in our manuscript and gave us the benefit of his advice. Peter had even begun a biography of Max and Monique Nemni, a project that was regrettably cut short by his sad passing on January 10, 2024.

We thank Russell Smith, our editor from Dundurn Press, and Peter Midgley, our copy editor, for their fine work on our manuscript. We thank, too, our colleague Meg Fox for her kind help diligently reviewing research notes and citations.

Finally, we wish to pay special tribute above all to our dear friend and colleague, Linda Hutcheon, whose editing, advice, and encouragement has been essential to our completing this book. Truly she has been a vital part of the team.

Notes

Unless otherwise indicated, French source material has been translated into English by the authors.

ONE Ottawa, Here I Come!

1 Pierre Elliott Trudeau, *Memoirs* (Toronto: McClelland & Stewart, 1993), 71.

2 Pierre Elliott Trudeau, "L'homme de gauche et les élections provinciales," *Cité libre*, November 1962, 4.

3 R. Pelletier, *Partis politiques et société québécoise: De Duplessis à Bourassa, 1944–1970* (Montreal: Québec/Amérique, 1989), 194–95.

4 Trudeau, "L'homme de gauche et les élections provinciales."

5 Pierre Godin, *Daniel Johnson, 1964–1968: La difficile recherche de l'égalité*, vol. 2 (Montreal: Les Éditions de l'Homme, 1980), 101.

6 *A Preliminary Report of the Royal Commission on Bilingualism and Biculturalism*, Appendix I, The Terms of Reference (Ottawa: Queen's Printer, 1965), 173.

7 *A Preliminary Report of the Royal Commission on Bilingualism and Biculturalism* (Ottawa: Queen's Printer, 1965), 13.

8 Max and Monique Nemni, *Young Trudeau, 1919–1944: Son of Quebec, Father of Canada*, vol. 1 (Toronto: McClelland & Stewart, 2006), 74.

9 Nemni, *Young Trudeau*, 308.

10 Martin Sullivan, *Mandate '68* (Toronto: Doubleday Canada, 1968), 105.

11 Sullivan, *Mandate '68*, 97.

12 Lester B. Pearson, *Mike: The Memoirs of the Right Honourable Lester B. Pearson*, eds. John Munroe and Alex Ingus, vol. 3, 1957–1968 (Toronto: University of Toronto Press, 1975), 218.

13 René Lévesque, *Memoirs*, trans. Philip Stratford (Toronto: McClelland & Stewart, 1986), 194.

14 Pierre Elliott Trudeau, "Some Obstacles to Democracy in Quebec," *Canadian Journal of Economics and Political Science* 24, no. 3 (August 1958).

15 Pierre Elliott Trudeau, "Pearson ou l'abdication de l'esprit," *Cité libre*, April 1963, cited in Max and Monique Nemni, *Trudeau Transformed, 1944–1965: The Shaping of a Statesman*, vol. 2, trans. George Tombs (Toronto: McClelland & Stewart, 2011), 451–52.

16 Pierre Elliott Trudeau, "Pearson ou l'abdication de l'esprit," quoted in Max and Monique Nemni, *Trudeau Transformed*, 452.

17 Sullivan, *Mandate '68*, 81.

18 Sullivan, *Mandate '68*, 116.

19 *Canadian Network for Research on Terrorism, Security, and Society*, Canadian Incident Database, tsas.ca/canadian-incident-database.

20 *Le Devoir*, June 6, 1966.

21 All references and quotes from the conference are taken from munkschool.utoronto.ca/mowatcentre/confederation-of-tomorrow-conference-1967-background-papers/.

22 Steve Paikin, *The Agenda*, TVO Transcript, December 12, 2017.

23 Paikin, *The Agenda*.

24 Government of Quebec, "Preliminary Statement," November 27–30, 1967. LAC Trudeau Fonds (MG26-020, Vol. 22, File 17), 14–22.

25 Gary Miedema, *For Canada's Sake: Public Religion, Centennial Celebrations, and the Re-Making of Canada in the 1960s* (Montreal: McGill-Queen's University Press, 2005), 68.

26 De Gaulle, quoted in Godin, *Daniel Johnson*, 2:219–23.

27 RG 2, Privy Council Office, Series A-5-a, vol. 6323, July 25, 1967.

28 Quoted in Pearson, *Mike: The Memoirs of the Right Honourable Lester B. Pearson*, 3:268.

29 *Le Devoir*, August 12, 1967.

30 Godin, *Daniel Johnson*, 2:356–61.

31 See the full story on French complicity in promoting Quebec separatism over three decades in William Johnson, "France and Canada: A History of Interference," *Cité libre*, English edition, April 1998.

32 Gary Kinsman and Patrizia Gentile, *"In the Interests of the State": The Anti-Gay, Anti-Lesbian National Security Campaign in Canada, a Preliminary Research Report* (Sudbury: Laurentian University, 1998).

33 John Ibbitson, "Trudeau Lags on LGBT Pardons," *Globe and Mail*, March 25, 2017.

34 While this saying is attributed to Trudeau, it is a paraphrase of the editorial of the *Globe and Mail* of December 12, 1967. Trudeau acknowledged it and thanked O'Malley.

35 W. Thorsell, "Sex, Drugs and Dying: You've Come a Long Way Canada," *Globe and Mail*, March 1, 2016.

36 Gary Kinsman, Dieter K. Buse, and Mercedes Steedman, eds., *Whose National Security? Canadian State Surveillance and the Creation of Enemies* (Toronto: Between the Lines, 2000), 49–50.

37 Kinsman, Buse, and Steedman, *Whose National Security?*, 63.

38 Kinsman, Buse, and Steedman, *Whose National Security?*, 30.

39 "Homosexual Law Sign of Decay Says Police Chief," *Toronto Daily Star*, December 23, 1967.

40 "Gabias Predicts Bill Will Lead to Decadence," *Globe and Mail*, December 29, 1967.

41 F.J.E. Jordan, "The Federal Divorce Act (1968) and the Constitution," *McGill Law Journal* 14, no. 2 (1968): 219.

42 Kristen Douglas, "Divorce Law in Canada," publications.gc.ca/collections/Collection-R/LoPBdP/CIR/963-c.htm.

43 *House of Commons Debates*, December 4, 1967, Vol. 5, 5017, in Jordan, "The Federal Divorce Act (1968) and the Constitution."

44 Lalonde, cited in R. Wright, *Trudeaumania: The Rise to Power of Pierre Elliott Trudeau* (Toronto: HarperCollins, 2016), 119.

45 *House of Commons Debates*, November 23–December 21, 1967, Vol. 5, 5455, 5457, 5458.

46 *Contraception, Divorce, Abortion, Three Statements by Canadian Catholic Conference* (Ottawa, August 1968), quoted in Andrew Thompson, "Slow to Leave the Bedrooms of the Nation: Trudeau and the Modernizing of Canadian Law, 1967–1969," in *The Hidden Pierre Elliott Trudeau: The Faith Behind the Politics*, eds. John English, Richard Gwyn, and P. Whitney Lackenbauer (Ottawa: Novalis, 2004), 123.

47 *House of Commons Debates*, Vol. 5, 5548.

48 CBC Television, *The Way It Is*, December 10, 1967, quoted in Paul Litt, *Trudeaumania* (Vancouver: UBC Press, 2018), 142.

49 J. Brodie, S.A.M. Gavignan, and J. Jansen, *The Politics of Abortion* (Toronto: Oxford University Press, 1992).

50 M. Coren, "Christians Are Obsessed with Abortion," in *Heresy: The Ten Lies They Spread About Christianity* (Toronto: McLelland & Stewart, 2012), 196–98.

51 M. Wilson, "Three Decades of Choice: Canada's Landmark Abortion Law Is 30 Years Old Tomorrow," *The Gazette*, May 13, 1999.

52 Wright, *Trudeaumania*, 121.

53 "Abortion Law Criminal, Say Filibusterers," *Ottawa Citizen*, May 6, 1969, 20.

54 Quoted in Wright, *Trudeaumania*, 121.

TWO Two Nations or One?

1 Daniel Johnson, *Equality or Independence*, ghost-written booklet, for Union Nationale, 1965, English translation, 14.

2 *Cité libre* remained dormant until 1990. It was revived after the failure of the Meech Lake Accord. From 1995 to 2000, Max and Monique Nemni were the directors and editors of the magazine.

3 Reported in W. Johnson, *A Canadian Myth: Quebec, Between Canada and the Illusion of Utopia* (Montreal: Robert Davies Publishing, 1994), 68.

4 "Déclaration de Johnson faite d'Hawai," *Le Devoir*, October 5, 1967.

5 "Pearson se réjouit," *Le Devoir*, October 5, 1967.

6 "À la longue, de Gaulle aura-t-il contribué à l'unité canadienne?," *La Presse*, October 6, 1967.

7 Pierre Duchesne, *Jacques Parizeau: Le croisé (1930–1970)*, vol. 1 (Montreal: Québec-Amérique, 2001), 424–32.

8 "Création du Mouvement souveraineté-association," Bilan Québec, August 20, 2024, perspective.usherbrooke.ca/bilan/quebec/evenements/.

9 "Option de la Fédération de SSJB: l'indépendance politique du Québec," *Le Devoir*, October 5, 1967.

10 Jules LeBlanc, "Rejet du fédéralisme et pleins pouvoirs au Québec," *Le Devoir*, November 27, 1967.

11 "Lesage: Trudeau ne reflète pas l'opinion qui prévaut au Québec. Le chef de l'opposition renouvelle l'offre d'une trève avec l'UN," *Le Devoir*, September 15, 1967.

12 "Texte de la déclaration du président de Gaulle sur le Canada," *Le Devoir*, November 28, 1967.

13 Paul Sauriol, "Les vues du général de Gaulle sur l'avenir du Canada français," editorial, *Le Devoir*, November 28, 1967.

14 In Wright, *Trudeaumania*, 102.

15 Canada, *Federalism for the Future: A Statement of Policy by the Government of Canada* (Ottawa: Queen's Printer, 1968), 2.

16 Canada, *Federalism for the Future*, 2.

17 Canada, *Federalism for the Future*, 2.

18 Canada, *Federalism for the Future*, 2.

19 Canada, *Federalism for the Future*, 6.

20 Canada, *Federalism for the Future*, 18.

21 Canada, *Federalism for the Future*, 22.

22 Canada, *Federalism for the Future*, 8.

23 Canada, *Federalism for the Future*, 11, 14, 15.

24 Canada, *Federalism for the Future*, 34.

25 *La Presse*, February 2, 1968.

26 Godin, *Daniel Johnson*, 2:317.

27 For a more detailed, and very interesting, historical perspective on the struggles between France, Quebec, and the federal government, including the Gabon incident, see J.L. Granatstein and R. Bothwell, "One Country or Two?," in *Pirouette: Pierre Trudeau and Canadian Foreign Policy* (Toronto: University of Toronto Press, 1991), 111–57.

28 Godin, *Daniel Johnson*, 2:315.

29 Godin, *Daniel Johnson*, 2:314.

30 P. Newman, "In TV Goldfish Bowl, They're All Good Guys," *The Toronto Star*, February 7, 1968.

31 Excerpts of Johnson's opening speech were reproduced in *Le Devoir*, February 7, 1968.

32 P. Gros d'Aillon, *Daniel Johnson: L'égalité avant l'indépendance* (Montreal: Éditions Internationales Stanké, 1979): 202, cited in Johnson, *A Canadian Myth*, 84.

33 Constitutional Conference, *Proceedings* (Ottawa: February 5–7, 1968), 223, primarydocuments.ca/constitutional-conference-proceedings-5-7-february-1968/.

34 Constitutional Conference, *Proceedings* (Ottawa: February 5–7, 1968), 219.

35 Constitutional Conference, *Proceedings* (Ottawa: February 5–7, 1968), 227.

36 Johnson, *A Canadian Myth*, 87.

37 Johnson, *A Canadian Myth*, 85, and in Robert Miller, "Put 'Special Status' to Voters, Joe Dares Johnson," *The Toronto Star*, February 6, 1968.

38 Constitutional Conference, *Proceedings* (Ottawa: February 5–7, 1968), 229.

39 Constitutional Conference, *Proceedings* (Ottawa: February 5–7, 1968), 229.

40 Constitutional Conference, *Proceedings* (Ottawa: February 5–7, 1968), 231.

41 Constitutional Conference, *Proceedings* (Ottawa: February 5–7, 1968), 233.

42 Constitutional Conference, *Proceedings* (Ottawa: February 5–7, 1968), 235–37.

43 Constitutional Conference, *Proceedings* (Ottawa: February 5–7, 1968), 237, 241.

44 Constitutional Conference, *Proceedings* (Ottawa: February 5–7, 1968), 241.

45 Constitutional Conference, *Proceedings* (Ottawa: February 5–7, 1968), 245.

46 Constitutional Conference, *Proceedings* (Ottawa: February 5–7, 1968), 247.

47 Constitutional Conference, *Proceedings* (Ottawa: February 5–7, 1968), 249.

48 Constitutional Conference, *Proceedings* (Ottawa: February 5–7, 1968), 249.

49 Godin, *Daniel Johnson*, 2:305.

50 Claude Ryan, "Le duel Johnson-Trudeau," *Le Devoir*, February 7, 1968.

51 René Lévesque, "La conférence constitutionnelle, l'amorce d'une vaste supercherie où les vrais intérêts du Québec n'étaient pas représentés," *Le Devoir*, February 12, 1968.

52 Granatstein and Bothwell, *Pirouette*, 135.

53 Frank Jones, "Trudeau, Johnson Clash over Special Status in Quebec," *Toronto Star*, February 7, 1968.

54 Godin, *Daniel Johnson*, 2:327.
55 Quoted in Wright, *Trudeaumania*, 194–95.
56 Godin, *Daniel Johnson*, 2:339.

THREE Three Years a Liberal: Presto! Prime Minister

1 Litt, *Trudeaumania*, 152.
2 John English, *Citizen of the World: The Life of Pierre Elliott Trudeau: vol 1, 1919–1968* (Montreal: Alfred A. Knopf, 2006), 449.
3 *Le Droit*, December 21, 1967, in Litt, *Trudeaumania*, 146.
4 Donald Peacock, *Journey to Power: The Story of a Canadian Election* (Toronto: The Ryerson Press, 1968), 186, cited in Wright, *Trudeaumania*, 136.
5 "Quebec Option," Wikimedia Foundation, fr.wikipedia.org/wiki/Option_Quebec.
6 Michel Vastel, *Trudeau le Québécois* (Montreal: Les Éditions de l'Homme,1989), 153.
7 G. Radwanski, *Trudeau* (New York: Taplinger, 1978), 98.
8 Radwanski, *Trudeau*, 100–101.
9 F. Jones, *Toronto Star*, January 23, 1968.
10 P. Newman, "Trudeau's Big Leap — Like Father Like Son," *Maclean's*, September 18, 2012.
11 Quoted in Litt, *Trudeaumania*, 156.
12 *Toronto Telegram*, in Godin, *Johnson*, 326.
13 C. Ryan, "Les deux événements du congrès libéral," *Le Devoir*, January 29, 1968.
14 G. Pelletier, *Years of Choice: 1960–1968*, trans. Alan Brown (Toronto: Methuen, 1987), 264–65.
15 Litt, *Trudeaumania*, 155.
16 Wright, *Trudeaumania*, 178n22, 336.
17 Radwanski, *Trudeau*, 40.
18 Radwanski, *Trudeau*, 101.
19 English, *Citizen*, 470.
20 Wright, *Trudeaumania*, 196.
21 Wright, *Trudeaumania*, 197.
22 Litt, *Trudeaumania*, 227. His references: John Saywell, ed., *Canadian Annual Review for 1968* (Toronto: University of Toronto Press, 1969), 27, 68.
23 Radwanski, *Trudeau*, 107.
24 Ramsay Cook, *The Teeth of Time: Remembering Pierre Elliott Trudeau* (Montreal: McGill-Queen's University Press, 2006), 75.
25 Quoted in Wright, *Trudeaumania*, 265.
26 Jean-Pierre Fournier, "Les grands défauts du débat: la durée, l'interprétation, la

grande solemnité," *Le Devoir*, June 10, 1968.

27 Wright, *Trudeaumania*, 265.

28 English, *Citizen*, 257.

29 Litt, *Trudeaumania*, 180. Litt gives many references who state the same thing but gives no further proof for their assertion.

30 Rutherford, in Litt, *Trudeaumania*, 180.

31 R. Shield, "TV for Two: With Trudeau It's Magic, Stanfield — Tragic," *Toronto Star*, May 27, 1968.

32 Quoted in English, *Citizen*, 257.

33 Litt, *Trudeaumania*, 179.

34 Litt, *Trudeaumania*, 186.

35 Peacock, *Journey to Power*, 256; Litt, *Trudeaumania*, 173.

36 Wright, *Trudeaumania*, 200.

37 "Most Canadians Want a Young English PM," *Toronto Star*, March 20, 1968.

38 Gilles Lesage, "Selon René Lévesque: Trudeau offre aux Québécois une 'joyeuse noyade' minoritaire," *Le Devoir*, April 11, 1968.

39 Lévesque, *Globe and Mail*, April 27, 1968.

40 Wright, *Trudeaumania*, 245–46.

41 Wright, *Trudeaumania*, 223–24. Pearson, *Mike*, 3: 332.

42 Trudeau, *Globe and Mail*, April 24, 1968.

43 Litt, *Trudeaumania*, 254.

44 "Trudeau Repudiates Ads on PC's 2-Nation Policy," *Globe and Mail*, June 20, 1968.

45 P. Newman, "The Facts and Fictions of the Trudeau Smears," *Toronto Star*, June 15, 1968.

46 Frank Howard, "Right-Wing Quebec Group Identifies PM with Communism, Perversion, Subversion," *Globe and Mail*, June 8, 1968.

47 "Slade Sees Red," *Globe and Mail*, June 15, 1968.

48 Wright, *Trudeaumania*, 253.

49 Dominique Clift, "Quebec Tories Use Crude Whispers About Homosexuality," *Toronto Daily Star*, June 14, 1968.

50 "Two Major Church Councils Denounce Attack on PM," *Toronto Star*, June 20, 1968.

51 John English, *Just Watch Me: The Life of Pierre Elliott Trudeau, vol. 2, 1968–2000* (Toronto: Knopf, 2009), 31.

52 Charles Taylor, "'Aura' Won't Last, Says a Pal," *Toronto Star*, April 24, 1968.

53 "Trudeau 'Obstacle to Unity': Cliche," *Toronto Star*, June 13, 1968.

54 George Bain, "A Matter of Sovereignty," *Globe and Mail*, May 10, 1968.

55 "Douglas: Unity Threat in PM's Quebec Stand," *Toronto Star*, May 11, 1968.

56 "Where Do the Tories Stand?" *Globe and Mail*, May 10, 1968.

57 Anthony Westell, "PM Warns Against Mistaking Views of Johnson for Quebec's," *Globe and Mail*, May 18, 1968.

58 Trudeau, *Toronto Star*, June 19, 1968, quoted in Wright, *Trudeaumania*, 263.

59 Fernand Beauregard, "Il n'y pas de problème québécois."

60 "Trudeau Hints He'd Lower Voting Age," *Toronto Star*, May 27, 1968.

61 Beauregard, "Il n'y pas de problème québécois."

62 Anthony Westell, "Wearing Stetson, Trudeau Urges Calgary to Individualism, Free Enterprise," *Globe and Mail*, June 19, 1968.

63 Geoffrey Stevens, "Trudeau Sounds Like a Conservative," *Globe and Mail*, May 22, 1968.

64 Lewis Seale, "PM Has Small c-Conservative Message for Ontario," *Globe and Mail*, May 27, 1968.

65 Lewis Seale, "PM Takes off Gloves, Rips into Separatists," *Globe and Mail*, May 28, 1968.

66 Frank Jones, "PM Shouts at Separatists," *Toronto Star*, June 7, 1968.

67 Vincent Price, "M. Trudeau et les chahuteurs," *Le Devoir*, June 10, 1968.

68 *Separatism: A Decade in Perspective*, directed by Ian McLaren (CBC: January 5, 1971).

69 Jules Falardeau, "Les 50 ans du Jour de la matraque," Tabloïd, June 21, 2018, 24heures.ca/2019/09/06/les-50-ans-du-jour-de-la-matraque.

70 Pierre Elliott Trudeau, *Mémoires politiques* (Montreal: Le Jour, 1993), 99.

FOUR Trudeau Launches the Just Society

1 Peter A. Cumming and Neil H. Mickenberg, eds., "Appendix VI: Speech by Prime Minister Trudeau," *Native Rights in Canada*, 2nd ed. (Toronto: Indian-Eskimo Association of Canada in association with General Pub. Co., 1971), 331.

2 Bob Joseph, *21 Things You May Not Know About the Indian Act: Helping Canadians Make Reconciliation with Indigenous Peoples a Reality* (Port Coquitlam, B.C.: Indigenous Relations Press, Page Two Books, 2018), 171.

3 Joseph, *21 Things You May Not Know About the Indian Act*, 172.

4 Sally M. Weaver, *Making Canadian Indian Policy: The Hidden Agenda 1968–70* (Toronto: University of Toronto Press, 1981), 63.

5 Weaver, *Making Canadian Indian Policy*, 72.

6 Lawrence Martin, *Chrétien: The Will to Win* (Toronto: Lester Publishing, 1995), 191–92.

7 Martin, *Chrétien*, 192.

8 See Alan C. Cairns, *Citizens Plus: Aboriginal Peoples and the Canadian State* (Vancouver: UBC Press, 2000), for a later comprehensive analysis of the Aboriginal Question.

9 H.B. Hawthorn, ed., *A Survey of the Contemporary Indians of Canada: Economic, Political, Educational Needs and Policies*, vol. 1 (Ottawa: Indian and Northern Affairs, October 1966), 6.

10 Hawthorn, ed., *A Survey of the Contemporary Indians of Canada*, 1: 6.

11 Hawthorn, ed., *A Survey of the Contemporary Indians of Canada*, 1: 11.

12 Hawthorn, ed., *A Survey of the Contemporary Indians of Canada*, 1:13.

13 Hawthorn, ed., *A Survey of the Contemporary Indians of Canada*, 1: 18.

14 Weaver, *Making Canadian Indian Policy*, 24.

15 Weaver, *Making Canadian Indian Policy*, 86.

16 Weaver, *Making Canadian Indian Policy*, 82.

17 Weaver, *Making Canadian Indian Policy*, 91.

18 Weaver, *Making Canadian Indian Policy*, 95.

19 Weaver, *Making Canadian Indian Policy*, 178.

20 Weaver, *Making Canadian Indian Policy*, 169.

21 *Statement of the Government of Canada on Indian Policy, 1969*, Department of Indian Affairs and Northern Development, 3, publications.gc.ca/collections/collection_2014/aadnc-aandc/R32-2469-eng.pdf.

22 *Statement of the Government of Canada*, 5.

23 *Statement of the Government of Canada*, 5, 6.

24 Joseph, *21 Things You May Not Know About the Indian Act*, 15.

25 See Andrew Stobo Sniderman and Douglas Sanderson (Amo Binashii), *Valley of the Birdtail: An Indian Reserve, a White Town, and the Road to Reconciliation* (Toronto: Harper Collins, 2022).

26 Stobo Sniderman and Sanderson, *Valley of the Birdtail*, 125.

27 Stobo Sniderman and Sanderson, *Valley of the Birdtail*, 127.

28 Weaver, *Making Canadian Indian Policy*, 183–87.

29 William I.C. Wuttinee, *Ruffled Feathers: Indians in Canadian Society* (Calgary: Bell Books, 1971), 2.

30 Wuttinee, *Ruffled Feathers*, 6.

31 Wuttinee, *Ruffled Feathers*, 10.

32 Weaver, *Making Canadian Indian Policy*, 174.

33 Weaver, *Making Canadian Indian Policy*, 177.

34 Peter McFarlane and Doreen Manuel, *Brotherhood to Nationhood: George Manuel and the Making of the Modern Indian Movement* (Toronto: Between the Lines, 2020), 109.

35 Weaver, *Making Canadian Indian Policy*, 180.

36 Weaver, *Making Canadian Indian Policy*, 170.

37 McFarlane and Manuel, *Brotherhood to Nationhood*, 120.

38 McFarlane and Manuel, *Brotherhood to Nationhood*, 106.
39 Harold Cardinal, *The Unjust Society* (Edmonton: Hurtig, 1969, 1.
40 Harold Cardinal, *The Unjust Society*, 2nd ed. (Toronto: Douglas and McIntyre, 1999), viii.
41 Cardinal, *The Unjust Society*, 3.
42 Cardinal, *The Unjust Society*, 7.
43 McFarlane and Manuel, *Brotherhood to Nationhood*, 117.
44 McFarlane and Manuel, *Brotherhood to Nationhood*, 117.

FIVE The Scourge of Political Violence in Quebec

1 "Just Watch Me," CBC Archives, also reported in D'Arcy Jenish, *The Making of the October Crisis: Canada's Long Nightmare of Terrorism at the Hands of the FLQ* (Toronto: Penguin Random House, 2018), 208.
2 Frantz Fanon, *The Wretched of the Earth*, trans. Constance Farrington (New York: Grove Press, 1963), 35.
3 D'Arcy Jenish, *The Making of the October Crisis,* 15.
4 These details of the kidnapping are those provided by James Cross himself and reported in Jenish, *The Making of the October Crisis*, 205–6.
5 Ryan Hamilton, "The October Crisis Remains a Haunting Moment in Canadian History," *Globe and Mail*, October 6, 2023. This remarkable article from a graduate researcher at Oxford University, based on recently declassified documents, sheds new light on the Cuban-Canada relationship during the October crisis.
6 Hamilton, "The October Crisis."
7 Hamilton, "The October Crisis."
8 Jenish, *The Making of the October Crisis*, 19.
9 Quoted in Jenish, *The Making of the October Crisis*, 20.
10 William Tetley, *The October Crisis, 1970: An Insider's View* (Montreal: McGill-Queen's University Press, 2010).
11 Jenish, *The Making of the October Crisis*, 23.
12 Jenish, *The Making of the October Crisis*, 30.
13 Jenish, *The Making of the October Crisis*, 32–37.
14 Jenish, *The Making of the October Crisis*, 41.
15 Jenish, *The Making of the October Crisis*, 41.
16 Jenish, *The Making of the October Crisis*, 88.
17 Jenish, *The Making of the October Crisis*, 87.
18 Jenish, *The Making of the October Crisis*, 115.

19 Jenish, *The Making of the October Crisis*, 115.
20 Jenish, *The Making of the October Crisis*, 225.
21 *La Cognée*, May 1964, quoted in in Jenish, 247.
22 *Victoire*, March 1969, quoted in Jenish, 247.
23 Duchesne, *Jacques Parizeau*, 1:566.
24 Guy Lachapelle, *La crise d'Octobre de 1970: La grande alliance René Lévesque et Claude Ryan* (Quebec City: Presses de l'Université Laval, 2020), 32. In *The October Crisis 1970*, William Tetley writes that the petition was generally called "the sixteen eminent personalities," 51.
25 Lévesque, quoted in *La Presse*, October 15, 1970.
26 Duchesne, *Jacques Parizeau*, 1:565.
27 Marcel Rioux, *Quebec in Question* (Toronto: Lorimer, 1978), 172.
28 Premier Robarts had issued a call for a "general war" against the FLQ and criticized the PQ.
29 Lévesque, *Memoirs*, 245.
30 *Le Devoir*, October 28, 1970.
31 Trudeau, *Memoirs*, 239.
32 Trudeau, *Memoirs*, 141. See also Jay Watz, special to the *New York Times*, November 2, 1970.
33 See Dominique Clément, "The October Crisis of 1970: Human Rights Abuses Under the War Measures Act," *Journal of Canadian Studies* 42, no. 2 (Spring 2008): 160–86.
34 *Cité libre* 28, no. 4 (Fall 2000).
35 *Cité libre* 28, no. 4 (Fall 2000): 44.
36 Tetley, *The October Crisis*, 104–5.
37 Frank Scott, in Tetley, *The October Crisis*, 107.
38 Tetley, *The October Crisis*, xix–xxv.
39 J.L. Granatstein, in Andrew Cohen and J.L. Granatstein, eds., *Trudeau's Shadow. The Life and Legacy of Pierre Elliott Trudeau* (Toronto: Random House, 1999), 298–99.
40 Pierre Trudeau, notes for a national broadcast, October 16, 1970, Library and Archives Canada, greatcanadianspeeches.ca.
41 Trudeau, *Memoirs*, 149–51.

SIX "Welcome to the 1980s"

1 Trudeau, *Memoirs*, 84.
2 Trudeau, *Memoirs*, 256.
3 Trudeau, *Memoirs*, 229.

4 L. Ian Macdonald, "1980 Referendum: Trudeau's 'Elliott' Speech a Turning Point in Canadian History," *Montreal Gazette*, May 14, 2020, montrealgazette.com/news/local-news/1980-referendum-trudeaus-elliott-speech-a-turning-point-in-canadian-history.

5 See the Table of 12 agenda items and the status of each in David Milne, *The Canadian Constitution: From Patriation to Meech Lake* (Toronto: Lorimer, 1989), 58–63.

6 Trudeau, quoted in Ron Graham, *The Last Act: Pierre Trudeau, The Gang of Eight and the Fight for Canada* (Toronto: Penguin Canada, 2011), 27.

7 Michael Kirby, *Report to Cabinet*, 1980. See David Milne, *The Canadian Constitution* (Toronto: Lorimer, 1991), chapter 3, 97–103, for a detailed review of the Kirby Memorandum.

8 Paul Gérin-Lajoie, *Constitutional Amendment in Canada* (Toronto: University of Toronto Press, 1950), 254. The author, later minister of education in Jean Lesage's government, was convinced such unilateralism would violate constitutional convention. We do not know what Trudeau's position was at that time.

9 Trudeau, *Memoirs*, 306.

10 Margaret Thatcher, quoted in Trudeau, *Memoirs*, 308.

11 See the many publications of eminent political scientist Alan Cairns for the ways in which the people's engagement with the Charter fostered a new understanding of their role as constitutional actors, of a new "ownership" of the Constitution, and changed their very consciousness as "charter Canadians."

12 Peter W. Hogg and Annika Wang, "The Special Joint Committee on the Constitution of Canada, 1980–81," *The Supreme Court Law Review* 81, no. 3 (2017): 3.

13 Hogg and Wang, "The Special Joint Committee on the Constitution of Canada," 23.

14 The article by Hogg and Wang is the best detailed review of the changes to the resolution, which evolved from the summer negotiations to the October 6 draft presented to Parliament, and finally to the complete approval of the amended resolution on April 23, 1981.

15 Hogg and Wang, "The Special Joint Committee on the Constitution of Canada," 18.

16 See David Milne, *The Canadian Constitution*, 24–34, for a brief review of the history of the amending formula discussions in Canada, complete with an historical table of amendment formulas.

17 Quoted in Ron Graham, *The Last Act*, 17.

18 Trudeau, *Memoirs*, 271.

19 Trudeau, *Memoirs*, 271–72. For an intensive analysis of this new federalism, see David Milne, *Tug of War: Ottawa and the Provinces Under Trudeau and Mulroney* (Toronto: Lorimer, 1986), illustrating a host of unilateral measures across several policy fields.

20 Trudeau, *Memoirs*, 306–7.

21 Quoted in David Milne, *The Canadian Constitution* (Toronto: Lorimer, 1991), 181.

22 Re: Resolution to Amend the Constitution, [1981] 1 S.C.R. 753, decisions.scc-csc.ca/scc-csc/scc-csc/en/item/2519/index.do.

23 Trudeau's full argument against the Supreme Court decision is set out in P. Trudeau, *Fatal Tilt: Speaking Out About Sovereignty* (Toronto: HarperCollins, 1991).

24 Pierre Elliott Trudeau, Convocation Speech at the Opening of the Bora Laskin Law Library, *The University of Toronto Law Journal* 41, no.3 (Summer 1991): 295–306.

25 Trudeau, *Memoirs*, 316.

26 Trudeau, *Memoirs*, 317.

27 Trudeau, *Memoirs*, 319.

28 Quoted in "The Charter at 40: An Historic Canadian Compromise," Policy Magazine, policymagazine.ca/the-charter-at-40-an-historic-canadian-compromise.

29 Levesque, quoted in Graham, *The Last Act*,

30 Trudeau, *Memoirs*, 326.

31 We have borrowed this clever title from a stimulating book written by consummate insiders on the constitutional train, and brain trust of Saskatchewan under Premier Alan Blakeney, authors Roy Romanow, Howard Leeson, and John Whyte, *Canada Notwithstanding: The Making of the Constitution, 1976–1982* (Toronto: Carswell Publishing, 2007).

32 *Canadian Charter of Rights and Freedoms*, s 33, Part I of the *Constitution Act*, 1982, being Schedule B to the *Canada Act 1982* (UK), 1982, c 11, (QL).

33 Trudeau, *Memoirs*, 323.

34 *Canadian Charter of Rights and Freedoms*, s 2, Part I of the *Constitution Act*, 1982, being Schedule B to the *Canada Act 1982* (UK), 1982, c 11, (QL).

35 *Canadian Charter of Rights and Freedoms*, s 7–8, Part I of the *Constitution Act*, 1982, being Schedule B to the *Canada Act 1982* (UK), 1982, c 11, (QL).

36 *Canadian Charter of Rights and Freedoms*, s 15, Part I of the *Constitution Act*, 1982, being Schedule B to the *Canada Act 1982* (UK), 1982, c 11, (QL).

37 Trudeau, *Memoirs*, 324.

38 Trudeau, *Memoirs*, 328.

39 Trudeau, *Memoirs*, 322.

SEVEN The Constitution "Forever and Ever"

1 Milne, *Tug of War*, 79.

2 Trudeau, *Memoirs*, 203.

3 Trudeau, *Memoirs*, 293.

4 Trudeau, *Memoirs*, 294.

5 See Lowell Murray, in *La Presse* and *Globe and Mail*, in Donald Johnson, ed., *With a Bang, Not a Whimper: Pierre Trudeau Speaks Out* (Toronto: Stoddart, 1988).

6 See Guy Laforest, "Trudeau and the Referendum," in *Trudeau and the End of a Canadian Dream* (Montreal: McGill-Queens University Press, 1995), 18.

7 Trudeau, quoted in Johnston, *With a Bang, Not a Whimper*, 57.

8 "1987 Constitutional Accord," Government of Canada, last modified October 5, 2021, canada.ca/en/intergovernmental-affairs/services/federation/1987-constitutional-accord.html.

9 Robert Bourassa, quoted in Ramsay Cook "Alice in Meechland," in Clive Thompson, ed., *Navigating Meech Lake: The 1987 Constitutional Accord* (Kingston: Queen's Quarterly and the Institute of Intergovernmental Relations, 1988), 59.

10 Pierre Trudeau, *Globe and Mail*, March 11, 1989.

11 Johnston's *With a Bang, Not a Whimper* contains both the newspaper article as well as Pierre Trudeau's presentation to the Joint Committee of the House of Commons and Senate.

12 Pierre Trudeau, cited in Johnston, *With a Bang, Not a Whimper*, 24–25. See David Milne for a fuller assessment of Bourassa's legacy and its impact on Pierre Elliott Trudeau in *Tug of War*, 48–56.

13 Guy LaForest, *Trudeau and the End of a Canadian Dream*, 4–7.

14 Trudeau's bold declaration indicated his preference for Machiavellian decisiveness over timid statesmanship.

15 David Milne, "Innovative Constitutional Processes: Renewal of Canada Conferences: January–March 1992," in Douglas Brown and Robert Young, eds., *Canada: The State of the Federation 1992* (Montreal: McGill-Queens University Press, 1992), 27–52.

16 See David Milne, "A Summary Overview," in Douglas Brown, Robert Young, and Dwight Herperger, eds., *Constitutional Commentaries: An Assessment of the 1991 Federal Proposals* (Kingston: Institute of Intergovernmental Relations, Queen's University, 1992), 17–34.

17 Pierre Elliott Trudeau, *Trudeau: "A Mess That Deserves a Big No": Pierre Elliott Trudeau's Historic Speech at the Eleventh Cite libré Dinner*, trans. George Tombs (Toronto: Robert Davies, 1992), 19.

18 Trudeau, *Trudeau: "A Mess that Deserves a Big No,"* 52.

19 Trudeau, *Trudeau: "A Mess that Deserves a Big No,"* 31.

EIGHT Conclusion

1 Yascha Mounk, *The Great Experiment: Why Diverse Democracies Fall Apart and How They Can Endure* (Toronto: Penguin Random House, 2022).

2 Nicolas Berdyaev, *Slavery and Freedom* (New York: Charles Scribner's Sons, 1944), quoted in Max and Monique Nemni, *Trudeau Transformed*, 71.

3 Kenneth McRoberts, *Misconceiving Canada: The Struggle for National Unity*, 2nd ed. (Toronto: Oxford University Press, 2019).

4 See Charles Taylor's argument for "deep diversity" and claims for collective or group rights against Trudeau's individual rights in *Multiculturalism and the Politics of Recognition* (Princeton: Princeton University Press, 1994). See also Charles Taylor, *Reconciling the Solitudes: Essays on Canadian Federalism and Nationalism*, ed. Guy Laforest (Montreal: McGill Queen's University Press, 1993).

5 See Mounk, *The Great Experiment* for further exploration of this term "groupism" and its characteristics, especially pages 92–94, 32–35.

6 See Guy Laforest, "The Meaning of Canadian Federalism in Quebec: Critical Reflections," dialnet.unirioja.es/descarga/articulo/3339980.pdf. See also Antoine Brousseau and Stéphane Savard, eds., *Contemporary Federalist Thought in Quebec: Historical Perspectives* (Montreal: McGill-Queens University Press, 2023).

7 See Max Nemni, "Two Solitudes, Two Nations, Two Illusions," *Cité libre*, 26, no. 3 (July 1998): 39.

8 Jacques Parizeau, translated and quoted by Max Nemni, from *Le Canada au seuil du siècle de l'abondance, entretiens de Cerisy-la-Salle 1968* (Montreal: HMH, 1969), 327, in "The Case Against Quebec Nationalism," *The American Review of Canadian Studies* 24, no. 2 (Summer 1994): 175.

9 Parizeau, *Le Canada au seuil du siècle de l'abondance*, 175.

10 Max Nemni, "The Case Against Quebec Nationalism," 176–77.

11 See A.I. Silver, *The French Canadian Idea of Confederation* (Toronto: University of Toronto Press, 1997).

12 McRoberts, *Misconceiving Canada*, 260.

13 See endnote 21 in chapter 2, confirming this recommendation of the B&B Report.

14 See Monique Nemni, "Nursing Linguistic Insecurity," *Cité libre*, 50th Anniversary 1950–2000, 28, no. 3 (Summer 2000): 26–33.

15 Pierre Trudeau, quoted in Thomas Axworthy and Pierre Trudeau, eds., *Towards a Just Society: The Trudeau Years* (Toronto: Penguin Canada, 1990), 361.

16 Pierre Trudeau, *Hansard*, April 15, 1980, quoted in Axworthy and Trudeau, *Towards a Just Society*, 290–91.

Index

About the Authors

MAX AND MONIQUE NEMNI CAME TO CANADA AS FRENCH-SPEAKING HISPANIC JEWS driven from Egypt after the establishment of Israel in 1948. Leaving Paris in 1956, they travelled to Canada as a virtually penniless honeymooning couple in a small compartment on a transatlantic cargo ship. Max first worked as an accountant and Monique as a secretary, but they each branched out into academic life — Max into political science and Monique into linguistics — and went on to teach in Ontario universities and in Quebec, where the Nemnis became friends with former prime minister Pierre Trudeau. After a stint serving as editors of *Cité libre*, Trudeau's journal espousing liberal ideas for Quebec, they secured his agreement to do his intellectual biography. The first volume, entitled *Young Trudeau* (McClelland and Stewart), came out in 2006, a prize-winning book that shockingly revealed Trudeau as a separatist and revolutionary in his youth. Their second volume, in 2011, entitled *Trudeau Transformed*, captured his exciting life of intellectual exploration and travel after the Second World War and his return to Quebec to fight against authoritarianism. More than a decade after this publication, Max Nemni teamed up with David Milne to complete their trilogy with volume three, *Trudeau as Statesman*.

DAVID MILNE, A PH.D. GRADUATE IN POLITICAL SCIENCE FROM THE UNIVERSITY OF Toronto in 1974, enjoyed interesting teaching and research careers on two islands: Prince Edward Island from 1970 to 1997 and the Mediterranean island of Malta from 1997 to 2015. Author of the bestseller *The Canadian*

Constitution (Lorimer, three editions), he has written or co-edited six books and numerous articles on Canadian and European politics. Building on his island experience, David's research and publications in this field with Godfrey Baldacchino have helped develop island studies as an accepted academic subject of enquiry.

His Ph.D. dissertation was an interdisciplinary journey into the field of architecture, city planning, and political theory under the supervision of constitutional expert Peter Russell. His travels to leading architectural sites and essays on architecture and politics have built upon this post-graduate work.

As for *Trudeau as Statesman*, it has been David's great joy to have joined his friends Max and Monique in bringing this final volume to completion.